A Tasteful

Reflection of

Historic

Rhode Island

Windows

Dining room window at Hammersmith Farm in Newport, Rhode Island.

This cookbook is a collection of favorite recipes,
which are not necessarily original recipes.

Published by Junior League of Rhode Island, Inc.

Copyright 1995 Junior League of Rhode Island, Inc.
21 Meeting Street
Providence, Rhode Island 02903
(401) 331-9302

Library of Congress Catalog Number: 95-61737
ISBN: 0-9648-450-0-8

Edited, Designed and Manufactured by
Favorite Recipes® Press
P.O. Box 305142
Nashville, Tennessee 37230
1 (800) 358-0560

Manufactured in the United States of America
First Printing: 1995   10,000 copies

Book Design by Thomas Wright Design

The proceeds realized from the sale of
Windows, A Tasteful Reflection of Historic Rhode Island
will be returned to the community through projects supported by
the Junior League of Rhode Island, Inc.

Cookbook Committee

Carolyn Palla Killian and **Patricia Lamy Smolley**, Co-Chairpersons

Leslie Ross Kellogg, Recipe Collection and Testing Chairperson

Amy Beth Simmons, Production Chairperson

Elaine Marie Colarusso, Marketing Chairperson

Committee Members

Melissa Bauer

Sherry Brown

Lisa Bruzzese

Ruth Clegg

Marguerite Crocker

Nancy Dorsey

Stephanie Healy

Mary Jacobs

Catherine Killian

Martha Lindstrom

Virginia Mead

Mindy Morley

Susan Petrocelli

Meg Rankin

Carol Yarnell

Dedication

Windows is dedicated to all volunteers, past and present, who have given unselfishly of their time, talent and treasure.

Junior League of Rhode Island

The Junior League of Rhode Island, Inc. is an organization of women committed to promoting voluntarism and to improving the community through the effective action and leadership of trained volunteers. Its purpose is exclusively educational and charitable. It reaches out to women of all races, religions and national origins who demonstrate an interest in and a commitment to voluntarism and to the community.

It has been estimated that during the past 75 years, members of the Junior League of Rhode Island have provided over 2.7 million hours of community service. To give you a peek into our window of history, the following is a very brief outline of those groups who have benefited from our commitment of time and/or financial support.

1920s

American Red Cross

Children's Friend Society

Federal Hill House

Girl Scouts of Rhode Island

Lying-In Hospital

Nickerson House

1930s

Campfire Girls

League of Women Voters

Rhode Island School of Design

St. Mary's Home for Children

Sophia Little Home

Traveler's Aid Society

1940s

Children's Symphony

Crippled Children & Adults of
   Rhode Island

Meeting Street School

Memorial Hospital of Rhode Island

National War Fund

Providence Tuberculosis League

Smith Hill Girl's Club

1950s

American Cancer Society

Children's Friend & Service

Family Service of Rhode Island

John Hope Community Center

Rhode Island Department of
   Mental Health

Urban League

1960s

Child Welfare Services

Juvenile Court Resource Center

Patrick O'Rourke Children's Center

Roger Williams Park and Zoo

1970s

Children's Rights Coalition

Philharmonic Youth Organization

Providence Journal Summertime Fund

Save the Bay

South Providence Tutorial

Volunteers in Action

1980s

Adolescent Pregnancy Child Watch

Dorcus Place

Providence Family Learning Center

Rhode Island Community Food Bank

Ronald McDonald House

Safe Kids

1990s and Beyond

Women's Resource Center of
   South County

Elderly Shelter Project

Hasbro's Children's Hospital

Project SVIC

The Tomorrow Fund

Acknowledgements

Historical Information:

Melissa Bauer and **Peter Lauro**, Research

Mark Archambeault and **Bill Metz**, Pettaquamsoutt Historical Society, South Kingstown, RI

Audobon Society of Rhode Island, Smithfield, RI

Henry L.P. Beckwith, Wickford Historian, North Kingstown, RI

Mary Bellagamba, Archivist, Middletown Historical Society, Middletown, RI

Regina Campbell, Bristol 4th of July Parade Coordinator, Bristol, RI

Central Falls Planning Department, Central Falls, RI

Cranston Historical Society, Sprague Mansion, Cranston, RI

Cumberland Public Library, Cumberland, RI

Max Dewardner, Owner, Yawgoo Valley Ski Area, Exeter, RI

Susan Erty, Communications Department, St. Georges School, Middletown, RI

General Stanton Inn, William Winegar, Charleston, RI

Greenville Public Library, Smithfield, RI

Jamestown Public Library, Jamestown, RI

Al Mattola, The Western Hotel, Nasonville, RI

Marion J. Mohr Memorial Library, Johnston, RI

Pat Murhtins, Historian, Burrillville, RI

Rhode Island Historical Society Library, Providence, RI

West Greenwich Public Library, West Greenwich, RI

Rita Lynch Wood, Portsmouth Historical Society, Portsmouth, RI

Wine Recommendations:

Elliott Fishbein, **Town Wine & Spirits**; **Susan Samson**, **Sakonnet Vineyards**

Contents

Introduction

It has been said that the eyes are the windows of one's soul. The cumulative eyes of the Junior League of Rhode Island's members—or the League's soul—have provided a vision of community service, of helping others, and of being a reliable source of assistance in the communities of which we are an integral part.

Windows is a tasteful reflection of historic Rhode Island and a celebration of the Junior League of Rhode Island's dedication to voluntarism and community service within Rhode Island and southern Massachusetts. The Junior League of Rhode Island has trained volunteers in the community for 75 years, with over 2.7 million hours of community service.

We chose windows as the theme for the cookbook because a window allows us to see two very different perspectives: we can look outward to our communities and their diverse populations and cultures abundant with cherished history, and from the same window, we can look inward to the League's extraordinary history of commitment, dedication, and giving.

Windows offers its readers a cornucopia of recipes, Rhode Island history, photographs and delightful tidbits about food and places in the state. There are some 250 kitchen-tested and tasted recipes that are easy to prepare. There are recommendations for wine selections for the main courses and pasta dishes. And there are recipe variations and suggestions for side dish accompaniments included throughout the book. In short, **Windows** is a reflection of people, of food, and of treasured history.

We hope you enjoy it, and that you will catch a small reflection of yourself within the pages.

A Tasteful

Reflection of

Historic

Rhode Island

Appetizers & Beverages

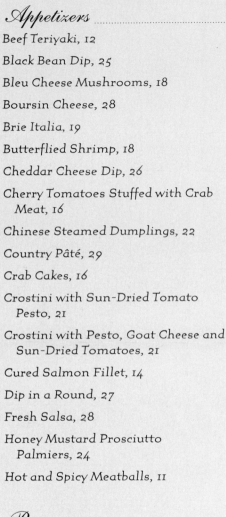

Appetizers

Beef Teriyaki, 12

Black Bean Dip, 25

Bleu Cheese Mushrooms, 18

Boursin Cheese, 28

Brie Italia, 19

Butterflied Shrimp, 18

Cheddar Cheese Dip, 26

Cherry Tomatoes Stuffed with Crab Meat, 16

Chinese Steamed Dumplings, 22

Country Pâté, 29

Crab Cakes, 16

Crostini with Sun-Dried Tomato Pesto, 21

Crostini with Pesto, Goat Cheese and Sun-Dried Tomatoes, 21

Cured Salmon Fillet, 14

Dip in a Round, 27

Fresh Salsa, 28

Honey Mustard Prosciutto Palmiers, 24

Hot and Spicy Meatballs, 11

Hot Brie and Chutney, 19

Italian Torta, 30

Jalapeño Cheese-Stuffed Finger Peppers, 20

Layered Pesto Spread, 30

Mussels in White Wine Cream Sauce, 17

Old-Time Cheese Spread, 31

Phyllo Cheese Triangles, 20

Pizza Dip, 27

Polenta con Quatro Formagi, 23

Roasted Garlic, 22

Smoked Salmon and Spinach Crepe Spirals, 13

Spinach Crepes, 13

Steamed Littleneck Clams Italian, 14

Sticky Chicken Wings, 12

Stuffed Quahogs, 15

Tomatoes with Pesto and Brie, 24

Ultimate Hot Crab Dip, 26

Warm Bleu Cheese Dip with Garlic and Bacon, 25

Beverages

Amaretto Coffee Creamer, 34

Bailey's Irish Cream, 33

Bavarian Mint Coffee Creamer, 34

Citrus Punch, 31

Mulled Wine, 32

Rum Runner, 33

Sprague Mansion Punch, 32

Tea Punch, 34

Hot and Spicy Meatballs

You may bake these meatballs at 350 degrees for 20 minutes instead of browning them in a skillet if preferred. They can be reheated to serve.

~ 3/4 cup catsup
~ 1/4 cup white vinegar
~ 1/2 cup water
~ 2 tablespoons brown sugar
~ 1 tablespoon minced onion
~ 2 tablespoons Worcestershire sauce

~ 3 drops of Tabasco sauce
~ 1 teaspoon dry mustard
~ 1/2 teaspoon salt
~ 1/2 teaspoon pepper
~ 12 ounces ground beef
~ 3/4 cup bread crumbs

~ 1 1/2 tablespoons minced onion
~ 1/2 teaspoon horseradish
~ 2 eggs, beaten
~ 3 drops of Tabasco sauce
~ 1/2 teaspoon MSG
~ 3/4 teaspoon salt
~ 1/2 teaspoon pepper

Combine the catsup, vinegar, water, brown sugar, one tablespoon onion, Worcestershire sauce, 3 drops of Tabasco sauce, dry mustard, 1/2 teaspoon salt and 1/2 teaspoon pepper in a sauté pan and mix well. Simmer until of the desired consistency. Mix the ground beef and bread crumbs in a bowl. Add 1 1/2 tablespoons onion, horseradish, eggs, 3 drops of Tabasco sauce, MSG, 3/4 teaspoon salt and 1/2 teaspoon pepper and mix well. Shape into 3/4-inch meatballs. Brown in a skillet, shaking to brown evenly. Drain the meatballs on paper towels. Add the meatballs to the sauce and cook until heated through. Serve warm. Yields 12 servings.

In 1663, King Charles II of England granted the Colony of Rhode Island and Providence Plantations the most liberal of all the colonial charters issued by the mother country. Characterizing the colony as a "lively experiment," the charter guaranteed "full liberty in religious concern-ments." The charter also established a self-governing colony with local autonomy and strengthened Rhode Island's territorial claims.

Beef Teriyaki

This is such an easy appetizer because the marinade can be prepared in advance, requiring no effort from the busy hostess.

- ~ 1/3 cup vegetable oil
- ~ 1/3 cup soy sauce
- ~ 1/4 cup sugar
- ~ 1/4 cup minced green onions
- ~ 3 cloves of garlic, minced
- ~ 2 tablespoons toasted sesame seeds (optional)
- ~ Tabasco sauce to taste
- ~ 1 flank steak

Combine the oil, soy sauce, sugar, green onions, garlic, sesame seeds and Tabasco sauce in a shallow dish and mix well. Slice the steak across the grain and add to the marinade. Marinate in the refrigerator for 3 hours or longer. Soak bamboo skewers in water. Thread the steak slices onto the skewers. Bake at 350 degrees until done to taste, turning once. Yields 8 servings.

Sticky Chicken Wings

Have plenty of napkins ready to serve with these easy finger-licking-good wings.

- ~ 3 pounds chicken wings
- ~ 1 cup packed brown sugar
- ~ 1 teaspoon mustard
- ~ 3/4 cup soy sauce
- ~ 1/4 teaspoon garlic powder
- ~ 1/8 teaspoon ground ginger

Cut each chicken wing into 3 portions, discarding the tips. Rinse the chicken and pat dry. Place in a large oblong baking dish. Combine the brown sugar, mustard, soy sauce, garlic powder and ginger in a bowl and mix well. Pour over the chicken. Bake at 350 degrees for one to 1 1/2 hours or until cooked through, turning once. Yields 12 servings.

Smoked Salmon and Spinach Crepe Spirals

The soft pastel colors of this dish make a beautiful presentation for bridal showers, engagement parties and wedding receptions.

~ Spinach Crepes (below)
~ 16 ounces cream cheese, softened
~ 1 tablespoon grated lemon zest
~ 2 shallots, finely minced
~ 1 tablespoon fresh lemon juice
~ 3 tablespoons chopped fresh dill
~ 2 teaspoons paprika
~ 2 tablespoons drained capers
~ 12 ounces smoked salmon, thinly sliced

Prepare the Spinach Crepes (recipe below). Beat the cream cheese in a mixer bowl until light and fluffy. Beat in the lemon zest, shallots, lemon juice, dill, paprika and capers. Arrange the crepes brown side up on a work surface. Spread each with 2 tablespoons of the cream cheese mixture and top with salmon slices. Roll the crepes tightly to enclose the filling and wrap with plastic wrap. Chill for 2 hours or longer. Trim the uneven ends of the rolls. Cut the rolls into 1/2-inch slices. Arrange on a serving plate. Yields 20 servings.

Spinach Crepes

~ 3 eggs
~ 1 1/2 cups milk
~ 1 cup flour
~ 1 bunch scallions, trimmed, minced
~ 1 (10-ounce) package frozen chopped spinach, thawed, drained
~ Dill, salt, cayenne pepper and black pepper to taste

Beat the eggs and milk at high speed in a mixing bowl for one minute. Add the flour and beat for one minute or until smooth. Stir in the scallions, spinach, dill, salt, cayenne pepper and black pepper. Add water if needed for desired consistency and mix well. Let stand for 15 minutes. Heat a 7- or 8-inch crepe pan over medium-high heat. Brush lightly with oil. Ladle 1/3 cup batter at a time into the heated pan and tilt to coat evenly. Bake for 2 minutes or until the bottom is light brown. Turn the crepe and cook for 30 seconds longer. Yields 10 crepes.

Rhode Island's
first permanent
settlement was
founded in 1636 by
Roger Williams,
who was banished
from the religiously
oppressive
Massachusetts Bay
Colony founded at
Boston in 1630.
Having a "sense of
God's merciful
providence unto me
in my distress,"
Williams "called the
place Providence."
He established the
settlement on the
concept of freedom
of religious thought,
making the colony a
refuge for several
persecuted religious

Cured Salmon Fillet

James Griffin and Christine Stamm of Johnson & Wales University, who contributed this recipe, tell us that it works best with a large salmon fillet, although you may reduce the recipe to use a smaller piece of fish.

~ 1 (3-pound)
boneless skin-on
salmon fillet

~ 2 cups sugar
~ 1 cup sea salt or
kosher salt
~ 1/2 cup chopped dill

~ 1 tablespoon pepper
~ Dill pickles and
capers, garnish

Place the salmon skin down in a nonreactive dish or pan. Combine the sugar, salt, dill and pepper in a bowl and mix well. Spread over the fish. Cure, uncovered, in the refrigerator for 20 hours. Scrape off any remaining sugar mixture carefully with a knife. Pat the fish clean and wrap in plastic. Chill until serving time. Slice the fish very thin and serve on toasted bread rounds. Garnish with chopped dill pickles and capers. Yields 20 servings.

Steamed Littleneck Clams Italian

Toasted garlic bread is good to soak up the delicious sauce from which these clams are steamed.

~ 1 medium onion,
chopped
~ 2 cloves of garlic,
minced
~ 1 tablespoon chopped
green chile peppers
~ 2/3 cup olive oil

~ 7 tablespoons white
wine
~ 1/4 cup tomato
sauce
~ 7 tablespoons water
~ Salt and pepper to
taste

~ 4 1/2 pounds
littleneck clams,
scrubbed
~ 16 slices toasted
French bread
~ 1/4 cup chopped
parsley

Sauté the onion, garlic and chile peppers lightly in the olive oil in a saucepan. Add the wine. Simmer until reduced by 1/2. Mix the tomato sauce with the water in a cup. Add to the saucepan with the salt and pepper. Simmer for 5 minutes. Add the clams and additional water if needed. Steam until the clams open. Arrange the toasted bread on a plate around a large serving bowl. Spoon the clams and cooking sauce into the large serving bowl. Sprinkle with the parsley. Yields 12 servings.

sects. This Rhode
Island concept
would form the
underpinnings for
the separation of
church and state.

Stuffed Quahogs

This is an excellent appetizer before a shore dinner; they are light and delicious, unlike some "stuffies" that are mostly bread. It is no more trouble to make a lot of these, so double the recipe and freeze the stuffed shells.

~ 15 pounds fresh quahogs (large clams)
~ 3 large onions, finely chopped
~ 1 cup packed chopped parsley

~ 1/2 cup butter
~ 1/4 cup flour
~ 2 egg yolks, beaten
~ Cayenne pepper and black pepper to taste
~ Worcestershire sauce to taste

~ Dried bread crumbs
~ Buttered bread crumbs seasoned with seasoning salt

Open the clams and remove the meat, reserving the liquid and shells. Wash the shells. Clam meat should measure about 4 cups and liquid should measure about 2 cups. Chop the meat in a food processor and combine with the onions and parsley in a bowl. Melt the butter in a large saucepan and stir in the flour. Cook for several minutes, stirring constantly. Stir in the reserved clam liquid gradually. Cook until thickened, stirring constantly. Stir a small amount of the hot mixture into the egg yolks; stir the egg yolks into the hot mixture. Cook for 5 minutes, stirring constantly. Add the clam mixture, cayenne pepper, black pepper and Worcestershire sauce and mix well. Remove from the heat. Add just enough dried bread crumbs to allow the mixture to hold its shape. Spoon into the reserved shells, rounding the tops. Sprinkle with the seasoned bread crumbs and place on a baking sheet. Bake at 400 degrees for 25 minutes. Serve hot. Yields 40 stuffies.

In 1638, Roger Williams established the first Baptist church in America. The First Baptist Meeting House, designed by Joseph Brown and constructed in 1775, stands at 75 North Main Street in Providence. It is a national historic landmark and is considered to be one of the finest examples of 18th century meeting house architecture in the country.

Crab Cakes

Serve appetizer crab cakes with mayonnaise flavored with orange and tarragon for dipping. They can also be made into larger cakes for a first course or luncheon.

~ 1 pound lump or snow crab meat
~ 1/4 cup mayonnaise
~ 2 tablespoons minced scallions
~ 1 egg, lightly beaten
~ 1/4 cup seasoned bread crumbs
~ 1/4 teaspoon Worcestershire sauce
~ 1 teaspoon dry mustard
~ 2 cups fresh bread crumbs
~ Vegetable oil for sautéing

Combine the crab meat, mayonnaise, scallions, egg, seasoned bread crumbs, Worcestershire sauce and dry mustard in a medium bowl and mix well. Shape by level tablespoonfuls into small balls and flatten into cakes. Coat well with the fresh bread crumbs, pressing firmly into surface. Sauté in heated oil in a large skillet until golden brown on both sides. Serve immediately or reheat at 350 degrees for 6 to 8 minutes.
Yields 16 small crab cakes.

Cherry Tomatoes Stuffed with Crab Meat

Cherry tomatoes are also delicious stuffed with Boursin Cheese (page 28) or Chicken Salad with Walnuts and Raisins (page 47).

~ 2 pints cherry tomatoes
~ 4 ounces cream cheese, softened
~ 4 ounces Montrachet or goat cheese, softened
~ 4 ounces snow crab meat
~ 1/2 red bell pepper, finely chopped
~ 1/2 green bell pepper, finely chopped
~ 1 scallion, finely chopped
~ 1/2 teaspoon chopped fresh dill
~ Finely chopped fresh parsley

Slice off the tops of the cherry tomatoes and scoop out the pulp. Invert onto a paper towel to drain. Process the cream cheese and Montrachet cheese in a food processor until smooth. Combine with the crab meat, bell peppers, scallion and dill in a bowl and mix gently. Spoon into the tomatoes and top with parsley. Chill until serving time.
Yields 24 to 36 tomatoes.

Mussels in White Wine Cream Sauce

Serve this with lots of French bread to soak up the delicious sauce.

~ 1 pound fresh
  mussels, scrubbed
~ 1 cup dry white wine
~ 1 teaspoon minced
  shallots
~ Juice of 1/2 lemon
~ 1 bay leaf

~ 1/2 teaspoon
  coarsely ground
  pepper
~ 2 tablespoons butter
~ 2 tablespoons olive
  oil

~ 1 teaspoon minced
  garlic
~ Salt and pepper to
  taste
~ 1/3 cup heavy cream
~ 1/4 cup chopped
  parsley

Combine the mussels with the wine, shallots, lemon juice, bay leaf and 1/2 teaspoon pepper in a large skillet. Simmer, covered, for 10 minutes or until the mussels open. Remove the mussels from the broth; strain the broth and reserve 1/4 cup. Separate the mussel meat from the shells, reserving the shells. Heat the butter, olive oil, garlic, salt and pepper in a skillet just until bubbly. Add the mussel meat and reserved broth. Bring to a boil and reduce the heat. Stir in the cream very gradually. Fold in the parsley and adjust the seasonings. Place the mussel meat in the reserved half shells and top with the sauce. Garnish with tiny sprigs of additional parsley. Serve immediately. Yields 6 servings.

The colony of Rhode Island was a leader in the American revolutionary movement. It openly defied British control, engaging in several acts of rebellion which predated the "shot heard round the world" in Lexington and Concord in 1775. In July of 1769 the British Customs sloop Liberty was scuttled in Newport Harbor, and in 1772, the British revenue schooner Gaspee was burned on Warwick's Namquit Point.

Butterflied Shrimp

This colorful dish has a Thai flavor and is especially attractive garnished with thin slices of radish and cucumber.

- ~ 20 uncooked large shrimp
- ~ 1/4 onion
- ~ 1 bay leaf
- ~ Salt to taste
- ~ 1 cup fresh lime juice

- ~ 6 tablespoons olive oil
- ~ 6 tablespoons soy sauce
- ~ 6 tablespoons Worcestershire sauce

- ~ 1 red onion, finely chopped
- ~ 1 to 3 jalapeño peppers, minced
- ~ Freshly ground pepper to taste

Fill a large saucepan 3/4 full with water and bring to a boil. Add the shrimp, 1/4 onion, bay leaf and salt. Cook for 3 to 5 minutes or just until the shrimp are pink and curl loosely. Drain and immerse in cold water. Let stand until cool. Drain and peel the shrimp. Butterfly the shrimp by making a deep lengthwise cut down the back, discarding the vein and opening the shrimp. Arrange flat on a serving plate. Sprinkle with the lime juice, olive oil, soy sauce, Worcestershire sauce, chopped onion, jalapeño pepper and ground pepper just before serving. *Yields 6 servings.*

Bleu Cheese Mushrooms

The bleu cheese in this stuffing introduces a new flavor to an old favorite. You can sprinkle some of the cheese on the stuffing if you prefer.

- ~ 12 to 14 large fresh mushrooms
- ~ 1/4 cup chopped green onions

- ~ 1/4 cup butter or margarine
- ~ 1 ounce bleu cheese, crumbled

- ~ Salt and pepper to taste
- ~ 1/3 cup fine dry bread crumbs

Remove and chop the mushroom stems, reserving the caps. Sauté the stems with the green onions in the butter in a skillet until tender but not brown. Stir in the cheese, salt, pepper and 2 tablespoons of the crumbs. Spoon into the reserved mushroom caps and sprinkle with the remaining crumbs. Place the mushrooms on a baking sheet. Bake at 350 degrees for 12 minutes. *Yields 6 to 8 servings.*

Hot Brie and Chutney

Serve this tempting easy dish on a frosty night by a warm fire.

~ 1 (9-ounce) jar
chutney
~ 1 (8-ounce) round
Brie cheese

~ 1/2 cup coarsely
chopped salted
roasted almonds

~ 2 tablespoons sliced
scallions

Cover the opened chutney jar with a paper towel. Microwave on Medium
for 1 1/2 to 2 minutes or until hot. Place the cheese in the center of a
9-inch microwave-safe serving plate with a rim. Microwave on Low for
4 to 4 1/2 minutes or just until it begins to melt. Stir the chutney and
pour over the cheese. Sprinkle with the almonds and scallions. Serve
warm with crackers or French bread. Yields 8 servings.

Brie Italia

Good recipes can also be simple, as this one proves. It is especially good
as an accompaniment for grilled beef, poultry or fish.

~ 1 (16-ounce) round
Brie cheese
~ 8 sun-dried
tomatoes, minced
~ 3 tablespoons
chopped fresh basil

~ 3 tablespoons
minced Italian
parsley
~ 3 cloves of garlic,
minced

~ 2 tablespoons
chopped pine nuts
~ 3 tablespoons
grated Italian cheese

Remove and discard the top rind from the Brie. Place on a serving plate.
Combine the sun-dried tomatoes, basil, parsley, garlic, pine nuts and
grated cheese in a bowl and mix well. Spread firmly over the Brie. Chill
for several hours. Let stand until room temperature before serving.
Serve with cracked wheat or other bland crackers. Yields 6 to 8 servings.

New Shoreham, or Block Island as the town is more popularly called, was settled in 1662. Housewives there were proud of their cheeses, derived from a Cheshire cheese recipe brought by early settlers from Glocester, England. Block Island cheese was proclaimed excellent by Benjamin Franklin, according to a thank-you letter he wrote to his lifelong friend, Catherine Ray Greene, wife of Rhode Island Governor William

Jalapeño Cheese-Stuffed Finger Peppers

You can vary the spiciness of this dish by substituting milder peppers for the pepperoncini. In either case, serve them with lots of cold beer.

- ~ 4 to 6 long mild Italian finger peppers
- ~ 1 cup chopped red bell pepper
- ~ 1 cup shredded jalapeño cheese
- ~ 1/2 cup chopped black olives
- ~ 1/2 cup chopped drained hot pepperoncini
- ~ 1/4 cup chopped scallions
- ~ 1/2 teaspoon minced garlic
- ~ 1 teaspoon kosher salt
- ~ 1/2 teaspoon coarsely ground pepper

Cut off and reserve the tops of the peppers, discarding the seeds and membranes. Combine the remaining ingredients in a bowl and mix well. Stuff carefully into the finger peppers. Replace the tops and secure with wooden picks. Place in a baking dish. Bake at 350 degrees for 30 minutes. Broil for one to 2 minutes or char lightly. Yields 4 to 6 servings.

Phyllo Cheese Triangles

Vary phyllo triangles by filling them with Warm Bleu Cheese Dip with Garlic and Bacon (page 25).

- ~ 4 cups shredded Monterey Jack cheese
- ~ 2 cups shredded sharp Cheddar cheese
- ~ 1/2 cup chopped fresh parsley
- ~ 2 eggs, beaten
- ~ Red pepper to taste
- ~ 1 (16-ounce) package frozen phyllo dough, thawed
- ~ 12 to 16 ounces melted butter

Combine the cheeses and parsley. Add the eggs and red pepper and mix well. Place one sheet of phyllo dough at a time on a work surface, leaving the remaining dough covered with a damp cloth. Cut the sheet into 3 1/2-inch strips. Brush with the melted butter. Place 2 teaspoons of the cheese mixture at the end of each strip and fold over to form a triangle. Continue to fold the dough flag-fashion to the end of each strip. Repeat with the remaining dough, butter and cheese mixture. Place the triangles seam side down on a baking sheet lined with baking parchment. Brush again with melted butter. Bake at 350 degrees for 20 minutes or until light brown. Remove from the pan and cool on a wire rack. Serve warm. Yields 36 appetizers.

**Greene. Mrs. Greene
had sent Franklin a
gift of Block Island
cheese, along with
some homemade
sugarplums.**
(Burke 99)

Crostini with Pesto, Goat Cheese and Sun-Dried Tomatoes

For variety, try using the Sun-Dried Tomato Pesto recipe that follows.

~ 2 cups fresh basil
   leaves
~ 2 cloves of
   garlic
~ 1 1/2 cups freshly
   grated Parmesan
   cheese

~ 2 1/2 tablespoons
   pine nuts
~ Salt to taste
~ 1/2 cup virgin olive
   oil
~ 1 loaf French bread,
   sliced 1/2 inch thick

~ 3/4 cup drained
   oil-pack sun-dried
   tomatoes, chopped
~ 3/4 cup chopped
   kalamata olives
~ 8 ounces goat
   cheese, crumbled

Process the basil and garlic in a food processor until smooth. Add the
Parmesan cheese, pine nuts and salt and process again. Add the oil
gradually, processing constantly. Spread on the bread slices and place
on a baking sheet. Layer the sun-dried tomatoes, olives and goat cheese
over the pesto. Broil 4 to 6 inches from the heat source for 3 to 4 minutes
or until the pesto begins to bubble and the cheese melts. You may toast
the bread lightly before spreading with the pesto if you prefer.
Yields 10 to 15 servings.

Crostini with Sun-Dried Tomato Pesto

This pesto is also delicious with pasta, poultry or fish.

~ 1 cup sun-dried
   tomatoes
~ 2 cups boiling water
~ 4 cloves of garlic
~ 1/4 cup pine nuts

~ 6 tablespoons
   parsley
~ 2 tablespoons basil
~ 2 tablespoons grated
   Parmesan cheese

~ 3 tablespoons olive
   oil
~ 1 loaf French bread,
   sliced

Soak the sun-dried tomatoes in the boiling water for 20 to 30 minutes or
until softened; drain. Combine with the garlic, pine nuts, parsley, basil,
cheese and olive oil in a food processor and process until finely chopped.
Chill until serving time. Serve with the French bread. You may use one
8-ounce jar of oil-pack sun-dried tomatoes if you prefer, reserving the oil
to thin the pesto. Yields 10 to 15 servings.

In June of 1775, the continental sloop Providence **won the first naval battle of the Revolution by capturing an armed tender of the** H.M.S. Rose. **The ship was built under the name of** Katy **by John Brown of Providence and was renamed** Providence **in 1774, when it became part of the original fleet of the United States Navy.**

Chinese Steamed Dumplings

Steamed dumplings are delicious served with a plum or duck sauce. They are just as good made with shrimp as pork.

- ~ 1/2 pound lean ground pork
- ~ 1 (8-ounce) can bamboo shoots, drained, finely chopped
- ~ 4 green onions, finely chopped
- ~ 1 egg white
- ~ 2 teaspoons soy sauce
- ~ 1/2 teaspoon grated fresh gingerroot
- ~ 1 teaspoon salt
- ~ 35 won ton skins

Combine the pork, bamboo shoots, green onions, egg white, soy sauce, gingerroot and salt in a bowl and mix well. Place one won ton skin at a time on a work surface, leaving the remaining skins covered with a damp towel. Place one heaping teaspoon of the pork mixture on each skin and bring the corners up to enclose the filling; press to seal. Arrange with sides not touching in a steamer sprayed with nonstick cooking spray. Steam for 20 minutes. Remove to a serving platter. Yields 35 dumplings.

Roasted Garlic

Roasted garlic has a sweet mellow flavor. Serve it as a spread for sliced baguettes or crisp crackers; it is a nice accompaniment for soups and salads.

- ~ 4 whole heads of garlic
- ~ 1/2 cup olive oil
- ~ Salt and pepper to taste

Slice the top 1/2 inch from the heads of garlic and discard some of the papery skins, leaving the heads intact. Place in a garlic baker or in the center of a large piece of foil. Drizzle with the olive oil and sprinkle with salt and pepper. Cover the baker or seal the foil packet. Bake at 275 degrees for one hour. Baste with the oil in the baker or foil. Cover and bake for one hour longer or until tender. To serve, squeeze the warm cloves of garlic out of their skins onto sliced bread and spread with a knife. Yields 6 to 8 servings.

Polenta con Quatro Formagi

Polenta squares are also delicious topped with roasted red peppers or wild mushrooms and served as a first course.

~ 2 quarts water
~ 3 tablespoons unsalted butter
~ 2 teaspoons salt
~ 3 cups finely ground yellow cornmeal
~ 6 ounces cream cheese, softened

~ 6 ounces Gorgonzola cheese, softened
~ 2 cloves of garlic, minced
~ 8 ounces mozzarella cheese, shredded
~ 3 ounces Parmesan cheese, grated

~ 3 tablespoons chopped fresh basil
~ Freshly ground pepper to taste
~ Olive oil for sautéing
~ 4 oil-pack sun-dried tomatoes, cut into thin slivers

Bring the water, butter and salt to a boil in a large saucepan over medium-high heat. Stir in the cornmeal very gradually with a wooden spoon. Reduce the heat to medium-low and cook for 15 to 20 minutes or until the mixture is thick and smooth and pulls away from the side of the pan, stirring constantly. Spread the mixture evenly in a buttered 10x15-inch baking pan. Cover and chill until firm. Combine the cream cheese and Gorgonzola cheese in a bowl and mix well. Add the garlic, mozzarella cheese and Parmesan cheese and mix well. Season with the basil and pepper. Cut the chilled polenta mixture into 1 1/2-inch squares. Sauté in a small amount of heated olive oil in a heavy skillet for 5 minutes or until light brown on both sides; drain. Arrange the squares on a baking sheet. Top with the cheese mixture, spreading as evenly as possible. Top each with a sliver of sun-dried tomato. Broil just until the cheese mixture is bubbly. Yields 48 squares.

Rhode Island renounced allegiance to King George III of England on May 4, 1776. It was the first of the thirteen colonies to do so, some eight weeks before the signing of the Declaration of Independence. The Rhode Island Assembly ratified the Declaration of Independence on July 18, 1776.

Honey Mustard Prosciutto Palmiers

These easy palmiers made with puff pastry would also be good filled with Sun-Dried Tomato Pesto (page 21).

~ 1 (11x18-inch) sheet frozen puff pastry, thawed

~ 3 to 4 tablespoons honey mustard
~ 6 ounces thinly sliced prosciutto

~ 1 cup freshly grated Parmesan cheese
~ 1 egg
~ 1 teaspoon water

Place the puff pastry sheet on a floured surface and spread with the honey mustard. Arrange the prosciutto over the mustard, covering the pastry completely. Sprinkle with the cheese. Roll the pastry from one side to the center, enclosing the filling. Roll from the opposite side in the same manner. Cut the roll into 1/2-inch slices. Place on baking sheets lined with baking parchment. Chill for 15 minutes. Beat the egg with the water in a small bowl. Brush over the palmiers. Bake at 350 degrees for 8 to 10 minutes or until puffed and brown. Yields 20 palmiers.

Tomatoes with Pesto and Brie

These tomatoes can also be prepared slightly in advance, then topped with the cheese just before serving and reheated in a 350-degree oven until the cheese melts. Top them with the pesto or serve it on the side.

~ 12 plum tomatoes
~ 2 cups packed fresh basil leaves
~ 3 cloves of garlic

~ 2 tablespoons pine nuts
~ 1/4 cup olive oil
~ 3/4 cup freshly grated Parmesan cheese

~ Salt and pepper to taste
~ 8 ounces Brie cheese, cut into 24 pieces

Cut the tomatoes lengthwise into halves and discard the seeds. Place cut side up on a greased baking sheet. Bake at 250 degrees for 2 to 2 1/2 hours or until most of the moisture has evaporated but the tomatoes are not completely dry. Process the basil, garlic, pine nuts, olive oil, Parmesan cheese, salt and pepper in a blender or food processor until smooth, scraping the side frequently. Top the hot tomatoes immediately with the Brie cheese. Top with the pesto mixture or serve it on the side. Yields 24 servings.

Black Bean Dip

Serve this easy dip with flour tortilla triangles or taco chips, Fresh Salsa (page 28) and icy Margaritas.

~ 1 (16-ounce) can
  black beans, drained
~ 1/4 cup (or less)
  olive oil

~ 2 tablespoons
  chopped fresh
  cilantro

~ 1 teaspoon chopped
  garlic
~ Kosher salt to taste
~ 1/4 teaspoon pepper

Place the beans in a food processor. Add the olive oil gradually, processing constantly until smooth. Add the cilantro, garlic, salt and pepper and process for 1 minute longer. Yields 8 servings.

Warm Bleu Cheese Dip with Garlic and Bacon

Reduce the fat and cholesterol in dips by using a small amount of a cheese with a strong flavor, such as bleu cheese.

~ 7 slices bacon,
  chopped
~ 2 cloves of garlic,
  minced
~ 8 ounces cream
  cheese, softened

~ 1/4 cup
  half-and-half
~ 4 ounces bleu cheese
~ 2 tablespoons
  chopped chives

~ Tabasco sauce to
  taste
~ 3 tablespoons finely
  chopped smoked
  almonds

Cook the bacon in a large heavy skillet over medium-high heat until nearly crisp. Drain the drippings from the skillet. Add the garlic. Cook until the bacon is crisp. Beat the cream cheese in a mixing bowl until light. Add the half-and-half and beat until smooth. Stir in the bacon mixture, bleu cheese, chives and Tabasco sauce. Spoon into a baking dish and cover with foil. Bake at 350 degrees for 30 minutes or until heated through. Sprinkle with the almonds. Bake, uncovered, until bubbly. Serve with crackers or vegetables. Yields 12 servings.

Cheddar Cheese Dip

This dip can also be spooned onto bread rounds or crackers and baked until puffed and golden brown.

~ 1 egg white
~ 3/4 cup mayonnaise
~ 1/2 teaspoon mustard
~ 1/2 teaspoon grated onion
~ Worcestershire sauce to taste
~ 1/2 teaspoon chopped parsley
~ 1 cup shredded sharp Cheddar cheese

Beat the egg white in a mixing bowl until stiff peaks form. Combine the mayonnaise, mustard, onion, Worcestershire sauce, parsley and cheese in a bowl and mix well. Fold gently into the egg white. Spoon into a small baking dish. Bake at 350 degrees for 30 minutes. Serve with crackers. Yields 4 to 6 servings.

Ultimate Hot Crab Dip

Serve this with Armenian bread, which can be found in specialty markets, such as the Near East Market in Cranston. Any unsalted cracker can be substituted for the Armenian bread.

~ 8 ounces cream cheese, softened
~ 1/2 cup sour cream
~ 1/2 cup shredded mozzarella cheese
~ 8 to 12 ounces fresh crab meat
~ 1 tablespoon lemon juice

Combine the cream cheese and sour cream in a mixing bowl and mix until smooth. Add the mozzarella cheese, crab meat and lemon juice, mixing well. Spoon into a small buttered baking dish. Bake at 350 degrees for 25 minutes. Serve with Armenian bread broken into small pieces. Yields 8 servings.

Dip in a Round

The "bowl" will be just as good as the dip in this recipe. It is also good with fresh vegetables.

~ 1 round loaf of bread
~ 8 ounces cream cheese, softened
~ 1/2 cup sour cream
~ 1/2 cup salsa
~ 2 cups shredded Cheddar cheese

Slice off the top of the bread and scoop out the center, reserving the top, bread and shell. Cut the bread into cubes. Combine the cream cheese, sour cream, salsa and Cheddar cheese in a bowl and mix well. Spoon into the bread shell. Replace the top of the bread. Wrap in foil and place on a baking sheet. Bake at 400 degrees for 1 1/2 hours. Serve with the reserved bread cubes for dipping. Yields 12 servings.

Pizza Dip

You will love this easy dip for party fare or couch potato evenings.

~ 8 ounces cream cheese, softened
~ 1/2 cup sour cream
~ 1 teaspoon oregano
~ 1/8 teaspoon garlic powder
~ 1/8 teaspoon crushed red pepper
~ 1 (8-ounce) can pizza sauce
~ 1/4 cup chopped green bell pepper
~ 1/4 cup chopped pepperoni
~ 1/4 cup chopped scallions
~ 1/2 cup shredded mozzarella cheese

Combine the cream cheese, sour cream, oregano, garlic powder and red pepper in a bowl and mix well. Spread in a 9-inch quiche dish. Top with the pizza sauce. Mix the green pepper, pepperoni and scallions in a bowl. Sprinkle over the pizza sauce. Bake at 400 degrees for 15 minutes. Sprinkle with the cheese and bake until the cheese melts. Serve with unsalted crackers or nacho chips. Yields 8 servings.

Rhode Island's
Revolutionary
War heroes include
Esek Hopkins,
first Commander
in Chief of
the Continental
Navy, and Nathaniel
Greene, General
and later
President George
Washington's
second-in-command
and Chief of the
Continental Army
in the South.

Fresh Salsa

Serve Fresh Salsa with blue tortilla chips or grilled quesadillas.

~ 3 or 4 tomatoes
~ 1 small Bermuda
onion, chopped
~ 1 green chile pepper,
chopped

~ 1 cup chopped
scallions
~ 1 green or red bell
pepper, chopped
~ 1/2 cup chopped
fresh cilantro

~ 3 or 4 cloves of
garlic, minced
~ 2 teaspoons kosher
salt
~ 1 teaspoon pepper
~ Juice of 1 lime

Slice the tomatoes into halves and gently squeeze out the juice and seeds;
chop fine. Combine with the onion, chile pepper, scallions, bell pepper,
cilantro, garlic, salt and pepper in a bowl and mix well. Add the lime juice
and stir. Chill for 30 minutes. You may also make this with 5 or 6 plum
tomatoes. Yields 8 servings.

Boursin Cheese

The flavors of this dip improve if it is allowed to age in the refrigerator
for three days.

~ 8 ounces cream
cheese, softened
~ 1/2 cup margarine,
softened

~ 2 cloves of garlic,
crushed
~ 1 teaspoon dried
tarragon

~ 1 teaspoon dried
chervil
~ 1 teaspoon dried
chives or parsley

Combine the cream cheese, margarine, garlic, tarragon, chervil and
chives in a blender, food processor or mixing bowl and mix well. Spoon
into a serving dish. Chill for 3 days. Serve with crackers or bite-size
vegetables. Yields 6 to 8 servings.

Country Pâté

This classic pâté is shared by James Griffin and Christine Stamm of Johnson & Wales University.

- ~ 8 ounces pork liver
- ~ 3/4 cup milk
- ~ 10 ounces ground pork
- ~ 8 ounces ground veal
- ~ 2 eggs
- ~ 8 ounces lean pork

- ~ 8 ounces pork fatback
- ~ 3 cloves of garlic, chopped
- ~ Grated zest of 1 orange
- ~ Salt and pepper to taste

- ~ 2 tablespoons brandy
- ~ 12 ounces sliced bacon
- ~ 3 juniper berries
- ~ 2 bay leaves
- ~ 1 teaspoon thyme
- ~ 1 teaspoon sage

Cut the pork liver into 1/2-inch pieces. Soak in the milk in a bowl for 8 hours. Combine the ground pork, ground veal and eggs in a bowl and mix well. Cut the lean pork and pork fatback into 1/2-inch pieces. Add to the ground pork mixture with the garlic, orange zest, salt, pepper and brandy. Drain the pork liver and discard the milk. Add the liver to the farce and mix well. Line the bottom of a terrine mold with the bacon strips. Pack the farce into the prepared mold. Top with the juniper berries, bay leaves, thyme and sage. Cover with oiled baking parchment. Place the mold in a water bath using a large baking pan. Bake at 350 degrees for 1 1/2 hours or to 165 degrees on a meat thermometer. Let stand until cool. Remove to a serving plate. Yields 20 servings.

Namquit Point, now called Gaspee Point in Warwick, was the site of one of the first overt acts of hostility against England, prior to the American Revolution. In March, 1772, the Gaspee, a British revenue cutter, was sent to enforce British customs regulations in Narragansett Bay. Overly zealous, the Gaspee and its crew were hated in Rhode Island. On June 9, 1772, the ship ran aground off Warwick. A

Italian Torta

The red, white and green colors of this cheese torta are particularly suited to holiday entertaining.

~ 20 ounces cream cheese, softened
~ 5 ounces Montrachet goat cheese without ash, softened

~ 3/4 cup unsalted butter, softened
~ 16 ounces Italian fontina or provolone cheese, sliced

~ 1 cup pesto
~ 12 oil-pack sun-dried tomatoes, drained
~ 1/3 cup pine nuts, lightly toasted

Line a 5x9-inch loaf pan with a double thickness of slightly dampened cheesecloth. Beat the cream cheese, goat cheese and butter in a mixing bowl until very smooth. Arrange a layer of the sliced cheese in the bottom of the prepared loaf pan, trimming to fit if necessary. Spread with a layer of the cheese mixture. Add a thin layer of the pesto and another layer of the sliced cheese. Spread with a layer of the cheese mixture and top with a layer of the tomatoes and a sprinkling of the pine nuts. Continue to layer in this sequence with the remaining ingredients, alternating the pesto and tomato layers. Cover the top with slightly dampened cheesecloth and press the torta gently to compress the layers. Chill for 8 hours or longer. Remove the cheesecloth from the top and unmold onto a serving platter, removing the cheesecloth liner. Arrange crackers or sliced French bread around the torta. Yields 25 to 30 servings.

Layered Pesto Spread

This simple recipe can be easily doubled or tripled for a crowd. It is convenient to make in advance or to transport to a party.

~ 1 (12-ounce) jar sliced sweet garlic peppers, drained

~ 8 ounces cream cheese, softened

~ 8 ounces prepared pesto

Cut the peppers into small pieces. Spread the cream cheese in a serving dish. Drain the pesto of any excess oil. Spread over the cream cheese. Arrange the peppers over the pesto. Serve with cracked pepper water crackers. Yields 6 to 8 servings.

Beverages

midnight plot was carried out by a group of 50 patriots who surprised the sleeping crew, taking control of the ship. After rowing the British to shore, the patriots set the Gaspee on fire. Despite a Royal investigation and the offer of a reward, no one would testify as a witness and no evidence was ever found. A Gaspee Days festival each June celebrates this patriotic act with a re-enactment of the ship burning.

Old-Time Cheese Spread

This easy spread is a perennial favorite. It can also be spread on crackers or bread rounds and broiled until puffed and golden brown.

~ 8 ounces sharp Cheddar cheese, shredded
~ 3 tablespoons milk

~ 2 tablespoons melted butter or margarine
~ 4 to 5 tablespoons dry sherry

~ 1 teaspoon dry mustard
~ Salt and pepper to taste

Combine the cheese, milk, butter, sherry, dry mustard, salt and pepper in a bowl and mix well. Pack into a crock. Chill in the refrigerator until firm. Let stand at room temperature before serving. Yields 8 servings.

Citrus Punch

You can enjoy this refreshing cooler any time of the year, but it is especially good with fresh strawberries in season.

~ 1 large can pineapple juice
~ 1 (12-ounce) can frozen orange juice concentrate, thawed

~ 1 (12-ounce) can frozen lemonade concentrate, thawed

~ 2 (10-ounce) packages frozen sliced strawberries
~ 1 quart ginger ale
~ 2 quarts soda water

Combine the pineapple juice, orange juice concentrate, lemonade concentrate and strawberries in a punch bowl and mix well. Add the ginger ale and soda water at serving time and mix gently. Yields 30 servings.

Cranston's Sprague Mansion was built around 1790 by the politically influential Sprague family, which produced two state governors. The Spragues owned an enormous cloth printworks empire worth nearly $20,000,000 at the time of the Civil War. Unfortunately, the Depression of 1873 caused the collapse of their business holdings, and the printworks and mansion were sold. The community

Sprague Mansion Punch

This modern version of the traditional Wassail bowl from the Sprague Mansion is served at the Cranston Historical Society's annual Christmas Open House, held to thank the community for their support in its purchase and restoration.

~ 3 cups sugar
~ 6 cups water
~ 6 ounces lemon juice

~ 1 (12-ounce) can frozen orange juice concentrate, thawed
~ 1 (46-ounce) can unsweetened orange juice

~ 4 bananas
~ 4 or 5 quarts 7-Up or Champagne

Dissolve the sugar in the water in a large container. Add the lemon juice, orange juice concentrate and orange juice and mix well. Purée the bananas one at a time with a small amount of the punch in a blender. Add to the remaining punch and mix well. Fill a mold with some of the punch mixture and freeze until firm. Chill the remaining punch. Unmold the frozen mold and place in a punch bowl. Pour in the punch and the 7-Up or Champagne and mix gently. Yields 40 servings.

Mulled Wine

Mulled wine was typical of the warming drinks served on cold days at Peleg Arnold's Tavern in Union Village, North Smithfield.

~ 1/2 cup sugar
~ 2 quarts red wine or dry white wine

~ 1 large navel orange
~ Whole cloves
~ 6 whole cinnamon sticks

~ 1/4 cup sugar (about)

Stir 1/2 cup sugar into the wine in a deep heavy kettle. Stud the orange with the cloves and add to the wine with the cinnamon sticks. Cook, covered, over medium heat until heated through, stirring occasionally; do not boil. Add water and additional sugar to taste. Serve hot in punch glasses or glass mugs with a garnish of a cinnamon stick or an orange slice. Yields 12 servings.

Beverages

supported the Cranston Historical Society in its campaign to save the mansion from demolition in 1967 and it is now home to the Society.

Bailey's Irish Cream

Bailey might have called this Southern Comfort Cream, as a nod to its foundation of bourbon.

~ 6 ounces sweetened condensed milk
~ 2 cups bourbon

~ 2 tablespoons chocolate fudge syrup
~ 2 tablespoons coconut cream

~ 1/4 teaspoon coconut extract
~ 2 cups whipping cream

Combine the condensed milk, bourbon, chocolate syrup, coconut cream and coconut extract in a blender and process until smooth. Add the whipping cream and process for one minute. Yields 8 servings.

Rum Runner

This refreshing drink from Key West, Florida, is a welcome addition to summer days and nights.

~ 7/8 ounce blackberry brandy
~ 7/8 ounce banana liqueur
~ 3/4 ounce 151 rum

~ 5/8 ounce grenadine
~ 1 1/2 ounces lime juice

Combine the brandy, liqueur, rum, grenadine and lime juice with ice in a blender and process until smooth. Yields 4 servings.

Beverages

The Providence Tea Party in Market Square took place in March of 1772, more than a year and a half before the Boston Tea Party of December, 1773. In May of 1774, the Providence Town Meeting became the first assemblage among the colonies to resist British policies, and in June, the General Assembly appointed Samuel Ward and Stephen Hopkins as delegates to the anticipated Continental Congress, making Rhode Island the first colony to do so.

Tea Punch

This recipe was shared by Lil Cumming, the Junior League of Rhode Island's President from 1951 to 1953. It can be served from a pitcher or punch bowl.

~ 4 cups water
~ 6 tea bags
~ 4 large sprigs of mint

~ 1 cup sugar
~ 3/4 cup (or more) orange juice

~ Juice of 1 lemon
~ 4 cups cold water

Bring 4 cups water to a boil in a saucepan and reduce the heat. Add the tea bags and mint. Simmer for 10 minutes. Remove from the heat and discard the tea bags and mint. Stir in the sugar until dissolved. Add enough orange juice to the lemon juice to measure one cup. Add to the punch with the cold water and mix well. Garnish servings with additional mint if desired. Yields 2 quarts.

Bavarian Mint Coffee Creamer

Package these coffee creamers in decorative tins or jars and decorate with ribbons for holiday giving.

~ 3/4 cup nondairy coffee creamer
~ 1/2 cup Dutch process cocoa
~ 3/4 cup confectioners' sugar

~ 1/2 teaspoon peppermint extract

Combine the coffee creamer, cocoa, confectioners' sugar and peppermint extract in an airtight container and shake to mix well. Use 2 tablespoons for each cup of coffee. Yields 16 servings.

Amaretto Coffee Creamer

~ 3/4 cup nondairy coffee creamer
~ 3/4 cup confectioners' sugar
~ 1 teaspoon cinnamon

~ 1 teaspoon almond extract

Combine the coffee creamer, confectioners' sugar, cinnamon and almond extract in an airtight container and shake to mix well. Use 2 tablespoons for each cup of coffee. Yields 12 servings.

A Tasteful

Reflection of

Historic

Rhode Island

Soups&Salads

Soups

Black Bean Soup, 37

Bouillabaisse, 45

Butternut Squash Soup, 38

Fennel Soup, 39

French Onion Soup, 40

Gazpacho, 40

Homemade Croutons, 46

Jambalaya, 46

Lentil Soup, 41

New England Fish Soup, 41

Pasta and Chicken Soup, 42

Rhode Island Clam Chowder, 38

Rouille, 45

Scallop and Gorgonzola Soup, 43

Sweet Red Pepper Bisque, 43

Wild Mushroom and Scallion
   Soup, 44

Salads

Broccoli Salad, 53

Caesar Salad, 53

Carrot and Pineapple
   Salad, 55

Celestial Salad, 54

Chicken Salad with Walnuts and
   Raisins, 47

Chinese Chicken Salad, 48

Citrus Coleslaw, 55

Cold Pea Salad, 58

Cranberry and Pineapple Mold, 47

Deluxe Turkey Salad, 49

Fresh Herb Salad Dressing, 62

Fresh Watercress Salad, 61

Frisée Salad with Minted Cucumber
   and Pink Grapefruit, 56

Grilled Salad Greens, 56

Mediterranean Potato Salad, 58

Mixed Green Salad with Pears and
   Bleu Cheese, 57

Pasta Salad, 50

Poppy Seed Salad Dressing, 62

Red Leaf Salad with Goat Cheese, 59

Spinach and Strawberry Salad, 59

Sweet and Sour Broccoli and
   Mushroom Salad, 52

Tomato Slices with Tabouli and Feta
   Vinaigrette, 60

Tortellini Salad, 51

Warm Spinach and Basil Salad, 61

Black Bean Soup

Serve bowls of sour cream, chopped plum tomatoes, chopped scallions, chopped red onion and jalapeño peppers for guests to garnish this hearty cold-weather soup. This recipe is from Leslie Kellogg of Leslie Kellogg Fine Foods.

~ 1 pound dried black beans
~ 7 cups water
~ 3 slices bacon, chopped
~ 3 medium yellow onions, chopped
~ 4 stalks celery with leaves, cut into 1-inch pieces

~ 4 carrots, cut into 1-inch pieces
~ 1 green bell pepper, coarsely chopped
~ 2 jalapeño peppers, minced
~ 3 cloves of garlic, chopped
~ 1 pound ham hocks or 1 ham bone

~ 3 cups beef broth, preferably homemade
~ 3 cups water
~ 1/2 cup sherry
~ 1/4 cup coarsely chopped cilantro
~ Salt and pepper to taste

Rinse and sort the beans. Combine the beans with 7 cups of water and bacon in a large saucepan and bring to a boil. Boil for 2 minutes and remove from the heat. Let stand, covered, during preparation of the broth. Combine the onions, celery, carrots, green pepper, jalapeño peppers, garlic, ham hocks, beef stock and 3 cups water in a large stockpot. Simmer, uncovered, for 1 1/2 hours. Strain through a coarse strainer and reserve only the broth. Drain the beans and add to the broth with any ham bones. Bring to a boil over medium-high heat. Reduce the heat and simmer, partially covered, for 1 1/2 hours or until the beans are tender; discard any bones. Process in several batches in a blender or food processor until smooth. Combine with the wine and cilantro in the saucepan. Add water as needed for the desired consistency. Simmer over medium heat until the flavors blend. Season with salt and pepper.

Yields 10 servings.

In coastal towns, the Native Americans had taught early settlers to prepare a feast called an Appanaug or clambake. An authentic Rhode Island clambake includes corn, onions, potatoes, sausages, steamers, fish and lobsters, which are covered with seaweed and steamed in a rock-filled firepit by a "bakemaster." Shore dinners may also include clam chowder, clam cakes, brown bread and watermelon.

Butternut Squash Soup

The advantage of this soup is that you can prepare it in advance, adding the cream as you reheat it at serving time.

~ 1 large yellow onion, thinly sliced
~ 1/4 cup butter
~ 48 ounces chicken broth

~ 1 cup unsweetened apple cider
~ 2 butternut squash, peeled, cubed

~ 1 cup heavy cream
~ 1 teaspoon curry powder

Sauté the onion in the melted butter in a skillet until translucent. Bring the chicken broth and cider to a boil in a stockpot. Add the sautéed onions and squash. Cook until tender. Process in a food processor until smooth. Return to the stockpot. Cook until heated through, stirring in the cream gradually. Add the curry powder just before serving. Garnish servings with parsley. Yields 6 servings.

Rhode Island Clam Chowder

This clam chowder is from Pauldon's Gourmet Express Catering.

~ 8 slices unsmoked bacon, cut into 1/2-inch pieces
~ 2 large onions, chopped
~ 8 stalks celery, chopped

~ 12 unpeeled small red potatoes, chopped
~ 3 quarts clam juice
~ 1 tablespoon marjoram

~ 1 tablespoon dill
~ Salt and pepper to taste
~ 1 quart shucked clams with juice

Cook the bacon in a skillet until the drippings are rendered. Drain, reserving 2 tablespoons of the drippings in the skillet. Add the onions and celery and sauté in the drippings over medium-high heat for 5 minutes. Combine with the potatoes, clam juice, marjoram, dill, salt and pepper in a large saucepan. Simmer, covered, until the potatoes are tender. Add the clams. Simmer over medium-high heat for 5 minutes; do not boil. Sprinkle servings with the bacon. Yields 16 servings.

Fennel Soup

It's a great soup and well worth the effort. Serve it with warm crusty French bread and a white Bordeaux or Sauvignon Blanc.

~ 1 1/2 tablespoons fennel seeds
~ 3 medium fennel bulbs, coarsely chopped
~ 4 large stalks celery, coarsely chopped
~ 3 medium onions, coarsely chopped
~ 3 tablespoons olive oil
~ 1 cup dry white wine
~ 3 quarts reduced-sodium chicken broth
~ 2 medium celery roots, or celeriac, peeled, coarsely chopped
~ 2 large russet potatoes, coarsely chopped
~ 1 clove of garlic, cut into halves horizontally
~ Bouquet garni of flat-leaf parsley, fresh thyme sprigs and bay leaf
~ Salt and pepper to taste
~ Fronds of 1 fennel bulb, chopped

Toast the fennel seeds in a skillet over medium heat for one minute or until fragrant. Grind in a mortar. Sauté the fennel bulbs, celery and onions in the heated olive oil in a large saucepan over medium-high heat for 7 minutes or until tender, stirring occasionally. Add the wine. Increase the heat and cook for 5 minutes or until the liquid has nearly evaporated. Add the chicken broth, celery roots, potatoes, garlic, bouquet garni and ground fennel seeds. Simmer for 45 to 60 minutes or until the vegetables are very tender. Discard the bouquet garni and garlic. Process the soup in a food processor until smooth. Press through a strainer into the saucepan and season with salt and pepper. Cook just until heated through. Top the servings with the chopped fennel fronds.
Yields 12 to 14 servings.

French Onion Soup

Line the bottom of the soup bowl with sliced Swiss cheese before adding the hot soup for an extra treat.

~ 2 cups thinly sliced onions
~ 2 teaspoons butter
~ 1 teaspoon flour
~ 3 cups beef broth
~ 8 slices French bread, lightly toasted
~ 1/2 cup shredded Swiss cheese
~ 1/2 cup grated Parmesan cheese

Sauté the onions in the butter in a saucepan until golden brown. Stir in the flour. Cook until bubbly. Add the beef broth. Simmer for 15 minutes, stirring occasionally. Ladle the soup into ovenproof bowls. Top each bowl with 2 slices of bread and sprinkle with the cheeses. Broil just until the cheeses melt. Yields 4 servings.

Gazpacho

Make gazpacho the day before and give the flavors time to blend for the best results.

~ 2 quarts plain or picante mixed vegetable juice
~ 1 red bell pepper, chopped
~ 1 yellow bell pepper, chopped
~ 1 green bell pepper, chopped
~ 6 plum tomatoes, seeded, chopped
~ 1 cucumber, seeded, chopped
~ 2 stalks celery, chopped
~ 1 sweet onion, chopped
~ 4 scallions, chopped
~ 1 small package radishes, chopped
~ Juice of 1 lemon
~ Juice of 1 lime
~ 2 tablespoons horseradish
~ Tabasco sauce to taste

Combine the mixed vegetable juice, bell peppers, tomatoes, cucumber, celery, onion, scallions, radishes, lemon juice and lime juice in a large bowl and mix well. Season with the horseradish and Tabasco sauce. Chill for 8 hours or longer. Yields 8 servings.

Lentil Soup

Corn bread is a good accompaniment for this hearty soup.

- 1 1/2 cups dried lentils
- 5 cups chicken broth
- 3 cups water
- 1 cup uncooked brown rice
- 1 (32-ounce) can tomatoes, chopped
- 3 carrots, sliced
- 1 onion, chopped
- 3 cloves of garlic, minced
- 1/2 teaspoon basil
- 1/2 teaspoon thyme
- 1/2 teaspoon oregano
- 1 bay leaf
- 2 tablespoons cider vinegar
- 1/2 cup chopped parsley
- Tabasco sauce to taste
- Salt, red pepper and black pepper to taste

Rinse and sort the lentils. Combine with the next eleven ingredients in a large saucepan. Cook for one hour. Add the vinegar, parsley, Tabasco sauce, salt, red pepper and black pepper and mix well. Cook for 30 minutes longer. Discard the bay leaf. Yields 8 servings.

New England Fish Soup

Use any firm white fish for this, such as pollack, scrod or perch. You may also add shrimp, scallops or other shellfish.

- 2 bay leaves
- 1/2 teaspoon dried thyme
- 1 teaspoon dried marjoram
- 1/2 teaspoon dried oregano
- 1 tablespoon salt
- 6 cups water
- 3 stalks celery, sliced
- 2 cups sliced carrots
- 1 small onion, cut into halves, sliced
- 1/2 cup chopped scallions
- 1/2 cup chopped fresh parsley
- 1 (28-ounce) can peeled whole plum tomatoes, crushed
- 1 teaspoon Tabasco sauce (optional)
- 2 pounds white fish fillets

Combine the bay leaves, thyme, marjoram, oregano, salt and water in a large saucepan. Bring to a simmer and add the vegetables and Tabasco sauce. Chop the fish or leave as fillets, which will flake as they cook. Add to the soup. Simmer, covered, for 30 minutes, skimming the surface as necessary. Discard the bay leaves before serving. Yields 4 to 6 servings.

Pasta and Chicken Soup

The herby flavor of this hearty soup is welcome on a cold winter night. Serve it with a salad and crusty bread.

~ 2 boneless skinless chicken breasts
~ 2 tablespoons olive oil
~ 1 large onion, finely chopped
~ 1 clove of garlic, minced
~ 1 red bell pepper, chopped
~ 3 1/2 cups chicken stock or broth
~ 1 (16-ounce) can tomatoes
~ 1/4 cup finely chopped fresh parsley
~ 3/4 teaspoon dried basil
~ 1/2 teaspoon dried oregano
~ 1 bay leaf
~ 1/4 teaspoon freshly ground pepper
~ 1 cup broken vermicelli or thin spaghetti

Cut the chicken into 1/2-inch cubes. Rinse and pat dry. Brown in the olive oil in a large saucepan or Dutch oven. Remove to a bowl with a slotted spoon. Add the onion, garlic and red pepper to the drippings and sauté until the onion is translucent, adding additional olive oil if needed. Add the chicken stock and undrained tomatoes, breaking up the tomatoes with a spoon. Return the chicken to the saucepan with the parsley, basil, oregano, bay leaf and pepper. Simmer, covered, for 5 minutes. Increase the heat and bring the soup to a boil. Stir in the pasta and reduce the heat. Simmer, covered, for 12 to 17 minutes or until pasta is tender. Discard the bay leaf. Serve with grated Parmesan cheese.
Yields 6 to 8 servings.

of the Shakespeare's Head." It also served as an important community gathering place in the 18th century, and housed the post office and the first book and stationery store in Providence. The property was acquired by The Shakespeare's Head Association, formed in 1937, and has been lovingly and faithfully restored and maintained, still serving its function as a meeting place.

Scallop and Gorgonzola Soup

Serve this with crusty French bread for a delicious summer meal. In the winter, substitute canned tomatoes and dried basil for the fresh ingredients.

~ 1 medium onion, chopped
~ 2 cloves of garlic, minced
~ 1 teaspoon butter
~ 1/4 cup fresh basil chopped
~ 4 to 6 fresh tomatoes, peeled, seeded, chopped
~ 1 tablespoon honey
~ 1 cup red wine
~ 8 ounces Gorgonzola cheese, crumbled
~ 8 ounces scallops, rinsed

Sauté the onion and garlic in the butter in a saucepan over medium heat until tender. Add the basil and sauté until wilted. Stir in the tomatoes, honey and wine. Simmer for 45 to 60 minutes. Adjust the seasonings Add the cheese and scallops. Cook for 5 to 10 minutes or just until the scallops are opaque. Yields 6 to 8 servings.

Sweet Red Pepper Bisque

This is a special soup contributed by a recent bride which was served at her wedding reception.

~ 1 small yellow onion, sliced
~ 1 tablespoon butter
~ 4 red bell peppers, cut into thin strips
~ 1 tomato, cut into quarters
~ 2 tablespoons uncooked brown rice
~ 2 tablespoons Cognac (optional)
~ 3 cups chicken stock or broth
~ 1/2 cup half-and-half
~ Salt, cayenne pepper and black pepper to taste
~ 1 tablespoon chopped parsley
~ 1/4 teaspoon paprika

Sauté the onion in the butter in a saucepan until tender. Add the bell peppers and tomato. Cook over medium-high heat for 5 minutes, stirring frequently. Add the rice and sauté for 5 minutes. Stir in the Cognac. Cook for 2 minutes. Stir in the chicken stock. Bring to a boil and reduce the heat. Simmer for 20 minutes. Stir in the half-and-half. Simmer over low heat for 20 minutes longer. Process in a blender or food processor until smooth. Strain into the saucepan and season with the salt, cayenne pepper and black pepper. Cook just until heated through. Top the servings with the parsley and paprika. Yields 2 to 4 servings.

Soups

Wild Mushroom and Scallion Soup

Thanks go to Chef Jaime D'Oliveira of the Capital Grille in Providence for this recipe.

~ 2 ounces dried mushrooms
~ 6 cups beef bouillon
~ 1/4 cup unsalted butter
~ 2 medium cloves of garlic, crushed

~ 3 bunches scallions, trimmed with 2 inches of greens, minced
~ Salt and freshly ground pepper to taste

~ 3 tablespoons flour
~ 1 cup heavy cream
~ 6 fresh mushroom caps, thinly sliced
~ 3 to 4 tablespoons finely minced parsley

Bring the dried mushrooms to a boil in the bouillon in a medium saucepan. Reduce the heat and simmer, covered, for 30 minutes or until the mushrooms are tender. Drain the mushrooms, reserving the broth. Mince the mushrooms. Melt the butter in a heavy-bottomed 3 1/4- to 4-quart saucepan. Add the garlic, scallions, 2 to 3 tablespoons of the reserved broth, salt and pepper. Simmer, covered, for 3 minutes or until very tender. Stir in the flour. Add the remaining reserved broth and whisk until well mixed. Add the reserved mushrooms. Bring to a boil and reduce the heat. Simmer, covered, for 20 minutes. Stir in the cream gradually. Cook just until heated through. Adjust the seasonings. Garnish the servings with thinly sliced fresh mushrooms and a sprinkle of parsley. Yields 6 servings.

Bouillabaisse

This is a specialty of the La France Restaurant.

- ~ 1/4 to 1/2 cup olive oil
- ~ 1/4 cup minced onion
- ~ White portion of 4 leeks, julienned
- ~ 4 medium tomatoes, peeled, chopped
- ~ 5 cloves of garlic, minced
- ~ 1 tablespoon chopped fresh fennel
- ~ 1/2 to 1 teaspoon saffron
- ~ 2 bay leaves, crushed
- ~ 1 teaspoon grated orange rind
- ~ 1/4 teaspoon celery seeds
- ~ 3 tablespoons chopped parsley
- ~ 1 teaspoon white pepper
- ~ Salt to taste
- ~ 2 tablespoons tomato paste
- ~ 2 cups white wine
- ~ 1/2 cup orange juice
- ~ 8 ounces scallops
- ~ 1 pound white fish fillets
- ~ 1 dozen each clams, mussels, oysters and peeled shrimp
- ~ Rouille (below)
- ~ Homemade Croutons (page 46)

Heat the olive oil in a large stockpot. Add the onion, leeks, tomatoes, garlic, fennel, saffron, bay leaves, orange rind, celery seeds, parsley, white pepper and salt. Sauté until the onion is translucent and the spices are aromatic. Stir in the tomato paste, wine and orange juice. Simmer until heated through. Add the scallops, fish, clams, mussels, oysters and shrimp. Simmer just until seafood is tender; do not overcook. Top servings with Rouille and Homemade Croutons. Yields 4 servings.

Rouille

- ~ 6 cloves of garlic
- ~ 1 egg yolk
- ~ 12 large basil leaves
- ~ 1/3 cup pimento
- ~ 1/3 cup fresh bread crumbs
- ~ Tabasco sauce to taste
- ~ 1 teaspoon salt
- ~ 1/2 cup olive oil

Process the garlic, egg yolk, basil, pimento, bread crumbs, Tabasco sauce and salt in a food processor until smooth. Add the olive oil very gradually, processing constantly at low speed until the mixture is the consistency of mayonnaise. Serve at room temperature. Yields 4 servings.

The Western Hotel, on the Providence to Douglas Turnpike in the Burrillville village of Nasonville, was established in the late 18th century as a stagecoach stop and tavern. At the beginning of the 20th century, water from a spring behind the hotel was used to make soda for the Nasonville Soda Works (McManus and Meade). Although the sodaworks closed in 1924, the Western Hotel continues to function as a roadside tavern and restaurant.

Jambalaya

Serve Sakonnet Vineyards Vidal Blanc and French bread with this spicy one-dish meal.

~ 1/2 cup chopped onion
~ 3 cloves of garlic, chopped
~ 3 tablespoons butter or margarine
~ 8 ounces andouille or kielbasa, cut into 1/2-inch pieces
~ 1 cup uncooked rice

~ 2 1/4 cups chicken broth
~ 2 medium potatoes, peeled, cut into 1/2-inch pieces
~ 1/2 cup dry white wine
~ 1 (4-ounce) jar sliced pimento

~ 1/2 teaspoon turmeric
~ Salt, cayenne pepper and black pepper to taste
~ 8 ounces uncooked large shrimp, peeled, deveined
~ 1/2 cup chopped fresh cilantro

Sauté the onion and garlic in the butter in a large heavy saucepan over medium heat for 5 minutes or until translucent. Add the sausage and cook for 5 minutes or just until it begins to brown. Stir in the rice. Add the chicken broth, potatoes, wine, undrained pimento, turmeric, salt, cayenne pepper and black pepper and mix well. Bring to a boil and reduce the heat to medium-low. Simmer, covered, for 20 minutes or until the rice and potatoes are tender and the liquid is absorbed. Stir in the shrimp and cilantro. Cook, covered, for 4 minutes or just until the shrimp are cooked through. Garnish with additional sprigs of cilantro.
Yields 4 servings.

Homemade Croutons

~ 2 tablespoons margarine, softened
~ 2 cloves of garlic, minced

~ 1 tablespoon minced parsley
~ Pepper to taste

~ 4 (3/4-inch) slices French bread

Melt the margarine with the garlic, parsley and pepper in a saucepan, stirring to mix well. Brush on both sides of each bread slice and place on a parchment-lined baking sheet. Bake at 350 degrees until crisp. Cut into cubes. Yields 4 servings.

Cranberry and Pineapple Mold

This salad is especially good with chicken, turkey and pork and is a nice addition to a holiday menu.

~ 1 (6-ounce) package any red gelatin
~ Chopped walnuts
~ 1 (16-ounce) can crushed pineapple
~ 1 (16-ounce) can whole cranberry sauce

Prepare the gelatin according to package directions, using 1/2 cup less cold water. Add the walnuts, pineapple and cranberry sauce and mix well. Spoon into a mold lined with cheesecloth. Chill for 2 hours or until set. Invert onto serving plate and remove the cheesecloth. Yields 10 servings.

Chicken Salad with Walnuts and Raisins

Serve this chicken salad in finger rolls with sugar snap peas and sun tea for a special luncheon.

~ 1 (3- to 4-pound) chicken
~ 3/4 cup mayonnaise or salad dressing
~ 3/4 cup sour cream or yogurt
~ 1/2 teaspoon ground ginger
~ Salt and freshly ground pepper to taste
~ 1/2 cup golden raisins
~ 1/2 cup broken walnuts
~ 1/4 cup chopped red bell pepper

Rinse the chicken well and combine with water to cover in a saucepan. Bring to a boil and reduce the heat. Simmer, covered, for one hour. Drain and let stand for one hour to cool. Cut the chicken into bite-sized pieces, discarding the skin and bones. Combine the mayonnaise, sour cream, ginger, salt and pepper in a bowl and mix well. Add the chicken, raisins, walnuts and bell pepper and mix gently. Chill until serving time. Yields 12 servings.

Chinese Chicken Salad

Carry this along for a summer picnic or outing on the boat. Add mandarin oranges or grapes for a summer luncheon.

- ~ 1 cup cashews or slivered almonds
- ~ 2 tablespoons sesame seeds
- ~ 1 can chow mein noodles
- ~ 2 cups chopped cooked chicken
- ~ 1 head lettuce, torn
- ~ 2 tablespoons chopped scallions
- ~ Chicken Salad Dressing (below)

Toast the cashews, sesame seeds and noodles in a moderate oven until golden brown. Cool to room temperature. Combine with the chicken, lettuce and scallions in a bowl. Add the dressing and mix well. You may substitute crisp-fried Chinese bean thread for the chow mein noodles and spice up the dressing with 1/2 teaspoon dry mustard if desired. Yields 4 servings.

Chicken Salad Dressing

- ~ 1/4 cup vegetable oil
- ~ 3 tablespoons rice vinegar
- ~ 2 tablespoons sugar
- ~ 1 teaspoon salt
- ~ 1/2 teaspoon pepper

Combine the oil, vinegar, sugar, salt and pepper in a small bowl and mix well. Chill until serving time. Yields 4 servings.

Deluxe Turkey Salad

This is a terrific luncheon dish served with Wild Rice and Pecans (page 152) and a salad of mixed greens.

~ 1 (6-pound) turkey breast
~ 2 (10-ounce) cans chicken broth
~ 2 cups water
~ 2 onions
~ 8 whole cloves
~ 1 stalk celery with leaves, chopped

~ 4 medium carrots, peeled
~ 1 bay leaf
~ 2 teaspoons salt
~ 10 whole peppercorns
~ Turkey Salad Dressing (below)
~ 2 cups mayonnaise

~ 1/2 cup light cream
~ 6 stalks celery, chopped
~ 2 (20-ounce) cans pineapple chunks, drained
~ 1/2 cup blanched whole almonds
~ Watercress

Rinse the turkey and pat it dry. Combine the chicken broth, water, onions studded with the cloves, celery, carrots, bay leaf, salt and peppercorns in an 8-quart saucepan. Bring to a boil and add the turkey. Return to a boil and reduce the heat. Simmer, covered, for 2 1/2 hours or until tender. Let stand for 1 1/2 hours or until cool enough to handle, basting frequently with the broth. Remove the turkey from the broth and cut into 1/2-inch slices and then into 3/4-inch pieces. Combine with the desired amount of dressing in a bowl; toss lightly to coat well. Chill, covered, for 1 hour or longer. Add the mayonnaise and cream and toss lightly. Fold in the celery and pineapple. Toast almonds in a 350-degree oven for 10 minutes or until golden brown. Sprinkle over the salad and garnish with watercress. Yields 12 servings.

Turkey Salad Dressing

~ 1/4 cup vegetable oil or olive oil
~ 1/2 cup lemon juice
~ 1 tablespoon onion juice

~ 2 1/2 teaspoons dried tarragon or 2 1/2 tablespoons chopped fresh tarragon

~ 3/4 cup chopped scallions
~ 1/4 cup chopped parsley
~ 1 teaspoon salt
~ 1/4 teaspoon pepper

Combine the oil, lemon juice, onion juice, tarragon, scallions, parsley, salt and pepper in a large bowl and mix well. Yields 2 cups.

Salads

Pasta Salad

The flavors in this salad improve with time, and it keeps especially well.

~ 2 cups fresh snow peas
~ 2 cups broccoli florets
~ 8 ounces cheese-filled tortellini

~ 3 ounces fettuccini, broken
~ 2 1/2 cups cherry tomato halves
~ 2 cups sliced mushrooms

~ 1 can pitted whole black olives, drained
~ 1 tablespoon grated Parmesan cheese
~ Pasta Salad Dressing (below)

Blanch the snow peas and broccoli for one minute. Cook the pasta al dente. Cool the hot vegetables and pasta. Combine with the tomatoes, mushrooms, olives, and cheese in a large bowl. Add the dressing and mix gently to coat well. Yields 6 servings.

Pasta Salad Dressing

~ 1/3 cup red wine vinegar
~ 1/3 cup vegetable oil
~ 1/3 cup olive oil
~ 1/2 teaspoon sugar
~ 1 1/2 teaspoons Dijon mustard

~ 1/2 cup sliced green onions
~ 2 tablespoons chopped fresh parsley
~ 2 cloves of garlic, minced

~ 2 teaspoons dried whole basil leaves
~ 2 teaspoons dillweed
~ 1/2 teaspoon oregano
~ 1 teaspoon salt
~ 1/2 teaspoon pepper

Combine the vinegar, oils, sugar, mustard, green onions, parsley, garlic, basil, dillweed, oregano, salt and pepper in a jar with a tight-fitting lid and shake to mix well. Yields 1 1/2 cups.

their home as an inn
and tavern during
the American
Revolution,
naming it after
Revolutionary War
General Joseph
Stanton. The inn,
open to the public
since this time, at
one point became
a major gambling
house and remained
one through the
Prohibition period.

Tortellini Salad

This is a great salad for your next cookout or picnic.

~ 1/2 cup chopped
walnuts
~ 16 ounces fresh or
frozen cheese- or
meat-filled tortellini
~ Salt to taste

~ 2 tablespoons olive
oil
~ 1/2 cup chopped
green onions
~ 2 red bell peppers,
chopped

~ 1/2 cup cured Italian
black olives,
drained, rinsed
~ 1/2 cup Tortellini
Salad Dressing
(below)
~ Pepper to taste

Spread the walnuts in a microwave-safe dish. Microwave on High for
4 minutes, stirring after 2 minutes. Cook fresh pasta in salted boiling
water for 5 to 10 minutes; cook frozen pasta for 10 to 15 minutes. Rinse
with cold water and drain well. Toss with the olive oil in a bowl and cool
to room temperature. Add the green onions, bell peppers, olives and
walnuts and mix well. Add 1/2 cup of the salad dressing and toss lightly
to coat. Season with salt and pepper. Chill until serving time. You may
add additional dressing at serving time if desired. Yields 6 servings.

Tortellini Salad Dressing

~ 1 cup olive oil or
1/2 cup olive oil and
1/2 cup vegetable oil
~ 1/3 cup wine vinegar
~ 2 teaspoons Dijon
mustard

~ 2 tablespoons
chopped fresh
parsley
~ 2 tablespoons
chopped fresh dill or
1 teaspoon dried
dillweed

~ 1 tablespoon fresh
oregano or
1 teaspoon dried
oregano, crushed
~ 1 teaspoon salt
~ 1/2 teaspoon freshly
ground pepper

Combine the olive oil, vinegar, mustard, parsley, dill, oregano, salt and
pepper in a bowl and mix well. Yields 1 1/2 cups.

Salads

Sweet and Sour Broccoli and Mushroom Salad

The dressing makes this vegetable salad a little different—a terrific addition to any buffet.

- ~ Florets of 1 large bunch of broccoli
- ~ 1 cup raisins
- ~ 1 cup sliced mushrooms
- ~ 1/2 cup chopped red onion
- ~ 6 slices bacon, crisp-fried, crumbled
- ~ Sweet and Sour Salad Dressing (below)

Combine the broccoli, raisins, mushrooms, onion and bacon in a salad bowl. Add the dressing and toss lightly or serve the dressing on the side if preferred. Yields 6 to 8 servings.

Sweet and Sour Salad Dressing

- ~ 1 egg
- ~ 1 egg yolk
- ~ 1/2 cup sugar
- ~ 1/2 teaspoon dry mustard
- ~ 1 1/2 teaspoons cornstarch
- ~ 1/4 teaspoon salt
- ~ 1/4 cup water
- ~ 1/4 cup white vinegar
- ~ 2 tablespoons butter or margarine
- ~ 1/2 cup mayonnaise

Whisk the egg, egg yolk, sugar, dry mustard, cornstarch and salt together in a bowl. Bring the water and vinegar to a boil in a saucepan. Whisk a small amount of the hot mixture into the egg mixture; whisk the egg mixture into the hot liquid. Cook until thickened, stirring constantly. Remove from the heat. Stir in the butter and mayonnaise. Chill, covered, in the refrigerator. Yields 1 3/4 cups.

Greene was a
Major-General and
second-in-command
of the Army, serving
directly under
George Washington.
Greene was a fine
strategist and
brilliant admini-
strator. He is
considered a hero
of the American
Revolution because
his excellent
Southern Campaign
in 1780—1781 set the
stage for the British
defeat at Yorktown.

Broccoli Salad

The green and red colors of this salad make it a nice addition to a holiday table.

~ 3 cups broccoli florets
~ 6 slices bacon, crisp-fried, crumbled
~ 1 cup chopped red onion
~ 1/2 cup shredded Cheddar cheese
~ 1/4 cup sunflower seeds (optional)
~ 1 cup mayonnaise
~ 2 tablespoons white vinegar
~ 1/4 cup sugar

Combine the broccoli, bacon, onion, cheese and sunflower seeds in a salad bowl. Combine the mayonnaise, vinegar and sugar in a small bowl and mix well. Add to the salad and toss to coat well. Chill, covered, until serving time. Yields 6 servings.

Caesar Salad

One secret to a good Caesar salad is to toss the lettuce with the dressing just before serving.

~ 1 large head or 2 small heads Romaine lettuce
~ 2 tablespoons light mayonnaise
~ 1 tablespoon Dijon mustard
~ 4 large anchovy fillets
~ 1 tablespoon minced garlic
~ 1 teaspoon Worcestershire sauce
~ 1 tablespoon red wine vinegar
~ 1/2 cup olive oil
~ 1 tablespoon fresh lemon juice
~ 1/4 teaspoon salt
~ 1/4 teaspoon freshly grated pepper
~ 1/2 cup grated Parmigiano-Reggiano cheese

Rinse the lettuce and pat it dry, discarding the outer leaves. Slice it crosswise. Combine the mayonnaise, mustard, anchovies, garlic, Worcestershire sauce and vinegar in a food processor and process until smooth. Add the oil gradually, processing constantly. Add the lemon juice, salt and pepper and mix well. Pour the dressing into a large salad bowl. Add the lettuce and toss lightly to coat well. Add the cheese just before serving. Garnish with croutons if desired. Yields 4 servings.

Celestial Salad

Dress up an Easter brunch or a spring or summer dinner with this beautiful salad.

- ~ 1/2 cup sliced almonds
- ~ 2 tablespoons sugar
- ~ 1 cup diagonally sliced celery
- ~ 2 green onions, sliced

- ~ 2 navel oranges, cut into 1-inch pieces
- ~ 1 avocado, chopped
- ~ 1 cucumber, peeled, chopped
- ~ 1 head Romaine lettuce, torn

- ~ 1 head leaf lettuce, torn
- ~ Celestial Salad Dressing (below)

Sprinkle the almonds and sugar in a small saucepan. Cook over medium heat until the sugar melts and coats the almonds, stirring constantly. Cool to room temperature. Combine the celery, green onion, oranges, avocado, cucumber, Romaine lettuce and leaf lettuce in a bowl and mix gently. Add the salad dressing and toss lightly to coat well. Top with the almonds. Yields 8 servings.

Celestial Salad Dressing

- ~ 1/4 cup olive oil
- ~ 1 tablespoon sugar
- ~ 2 tablespoons white vinegar

- ~ 1/2 teaspoon red wine vinegar
- ~ Red pepper sauce to taste

- ~ 1/2 teaspoon salt
- ~ Pepper to taste

Combine the olive oil, sugar, vinegars, pepper sauce, salt and pepper in a bowl and whisk until smooth. Store in the refrigerator. Yields 1/2 cup.

Carrot and Pineapple Salad

The presentation of this salad makes it an attractive addition to a summer barbecue or patio party.

~ 1 1/2 pounds carrots, shredded or julienned
~ 1/2 fresh pineapple
~ 3 tablespoons chopped scallions

~ 1/4 cup olive oil
~ 2 tablespoons lemon juice
~ 1 teaspoon honey
~ 2 teaspoons Dijon mustard

~ White pepper to taste
~ 3 tablespoons chopped parsley

Steam the carrots for 6 to 8 minutes or just until tender. Chill in the refrigerator. Scoop the pulp from the pineapple half, leaving the shell intact. Chop the pulp. Combine with the carrots and scallions in a bowl. Whisk together the olive oil, lemon juice, honey, mustard and white pepper in a bowl. Add to the pineapple mixture and mix gently. Spoon into the pineapple shell and sprinkle with the parsley. Chill until serving time. Yields 6 servings.

Citrus Coleslaw

Dieters will appreciate this tasty low-fat salad. It is even easier made with coleslaw mix and canned mandarin oranges.

~ 1/2 cup low-fat orange yogurt
~ 1 tablespoon skim milk

~ 1/8 teaspoon ground ginger
~ 3 cups shredded cabbage

~ 1/2 cup shredded carrots
~ 1 cup fresh orange sections

Combine the yogurt, skim milk and ginger in a bowl and mix well. Add the mixture to the cabbage, carrots and oranges in a bowl and toss lightly to coat. Yields 4 servings.

William Blackstone, Boston's first settler, left Boston in 1635 because of religious intolerance and moved to what is now Cumberland, becoming the first white settler in Rhode Island. Cumberland, "the mineral pocket of New England," has a great variety of minerals, including gold, copper, iron, coal and cumberlandite, a rare mineral with magnetic properties that is not found

Frisée Salad with Minted Cucumber and Pink Grapefruit

Chef Louise Wilcox of Citizens Bank contributes this light and delightful salad.

~ English cucumber, chopped
~ Chopped fresh mint
~ Baby frisée
~ Chopped pink grapefruit sections
~ Toasted walnuts

~ Grated Gruyère cheese
~ 1/4 cup lemon juice
~ 1/4 cup cider vinegar
~ 1/4 cup seltzer water or Champagne

~ 1/2 cup chicken broth
~ 3 tablespoons fresh oregano
~ 2 tablespoons fresh rosemary
~ 2 cloves of garlic

Sprinkle the cucumber with mint and let stand for several minutes. Combine with the lettuce in a bowl and toss lightly. Spoon into the center of a serving platter. Surround with the grapefruit. Sprinkle with walnuts and Gruyère cheese. Blend the lemon juice, vinegar, seltzer water, chicken broth, oregano, rosemary and garlic in a blender and process until smooth. Drizzle over the salad. Yields 1 1/2 cups salad dressing.

Grilled Salad Greens

This is an unusual and colorful accompaniment to any meal.

~ 1 head radicchio
~ 1 small head chicory
~ 3 small heads endive
~ Olive oil

~ 1 clove of garlic, minced
~ 1 1/2 teaspoons salt
~ 1 teaspoon pepper

~ 1/2 cup roasted whole red pepper, sliced
~ 3 tablespoons balsamic vinegar

Cut the radicchio, chicory and endive heads into halves. Brush the cut sides with olive oil and sprinkle with garlic, salt and pepper. Place cut side down on heated grill over medium-hot coals. Grill, covered, for 4 to 5 minutes. Arrange on large serving platter. Arrange pepper over the top. Sprinkle with the vinegar and serve immediately. Yields 6 servings.

Salads

anywhere else
in the world.
Gemstones such as
garnet, hematite
and malachite have
been found in the
area as well.

Mixed Green Salad with Pears and Bleu Cheese

The combination of the pears and greens with the bleu cheese is attractive as well as delicious. It would also be good with other fruit.

~ 3 unpeeled Bartlett pears, sliced
~ Lemon juice
~ Lemon Vinaigrette (below)

~ 1 head curly green lettuce, endive, radicchio or other salad greens

~ 1/2 cup crumbled bleu cheese
~ 1/2 cup chopped walnuts

Dip the pear slices in lemon juice to prevent browning. Add enough Lemon Vinaigrette to the salad greens to coat and toss lightly in a bowl. Spoon onto a platter or individual serving plates. Arrange the pears over the greens and sprinkle with the bleu cheese and walnuts. Serve with additional salad dressing. Yields 6 servings.

Lemon Vinaigrette

~ 1/2 cup olive oil
~ 1/4 cup fresh lemon juice
~ 1 teaspoon minced garlic

~ 1 tablespoon minced fresh parsley
~ 1 teaspoon Dijon mustard

~ 1 teaspoon kosher salt
~ 1/2 teaspoon freshly ground pepper

Combine the olive oil, lemon juice, garlic, parsley, mustard, salt and pepper in a bowl and whisk until smooth. Yields 3/4 cup.

Salads

Crescent Park, on the East Providence shore, was one of New England's premier recreational attractions. Appealing to the area's bustling summer colony, the park opened in 1886. Crowds of over 75,000 vacationers and daytrippers would come on the weekends in the park's heyday to enjoy the dance halls, dining rooms, roller coaster and carousels. Although the park closed in recent years, the elaborate 66-horse steam-powered

Cold Pea Salad

Try this quick salad for a refreshing summer salad. Substitute macadamia nuts or sunflower seeds for the cashews for a change.

- ~ 1 (10-ounce) package frozen peas
- ~ 1 cup chopped celery
- ~ 1/4 cup chopped scallions
- ~ 1 teaspoon chopped fresh dill or 1/4 teaspoon dried dill
- ~ 1/2 cup sour cream
- ~ 1 cup cashews

Combine the peas, celery, scallions and dill in a bowl. Add the sour cream and mix well. Chill until serving time. Add the cashews just before serving. Yields 4 to 6 servings.

Mediterranean Potato Salad

Make this salad in the summer when vine-ripened tomatoes are at their peak.

- ~ 1 pound potatoes, peeled, coarsely chopped
- ~ Salt to taste
- ~ 1 pound ripe tomatoes, seeded, coarsely chopped
- ~ 1/4 red onion, sliced
- ~ 1 1/2 cups medium black olives
- ~ 2 to 3 tablespoons capers
- ~ 1 tablespoon red wine vinegar
- ~ 1/4 cup extra-virgin olive oil
- ~ 1 to 2 teaspoons dried oregano
- ~ Pepper to taste

Cook the potatoes in enough salted water to cover in a large saucepan until tender. Drain and cool slightly. Combine the potatoes with the tomatoes, onion, olives and capers in a large bowl and mix well. Add the vinegar, olive oil, oregano, salt and pepper and toss lightly to coat. Yields 4 servings.

wooden carousel has been preserved and is recognized as one of the finest of its type in the country.

Red Leaf Salad with Goat Cheese

Arrange this simple salad on a serving platter for an attractive presentation.

~ Pine nuts
~ 1 head red leaf lettuce, torn
~ 1 package goat cheese, chopped

~ 1 jar oil-pack sun-dried tomatoes, chopped
~ Balsamic vinegar
~ Olive oil

~ Salt and pepper to taste

Spread the pine nuts on a baking sheet. Bake at 200 degrees for one hour, stirring several times. Combine the lettuce, cheese, sun-dried tomatoes and pine nuts in a bowl and mix well. Add vinegar, olive oil, salt and pepper. Yields 6 servings.

Spinach and Strawberry Salad

Enjoy this salad when strawberries are at their peak. It can be made with mandarin oranges when strawberries are not in season. Top it with caramelized pecans for special occasions.

~ 1 pound fresh spinach, torn
~ 1 quart strawberries, sliced
~ 1/4 cup red wine vinegar

~ 1/2 cup vegetable oil
~ 1/4 teaspoon Worcestershire sauce
~ 1 1/2 teaspoons grated onion

~ 1/4 cup sugar
~ 1 tablespoon poppy seeds
~ 2 tablespoons sesame seeds

Combine the spinach and strawberries in a large salad bowl and mix lightly. Combine the vinegar, oil, Worcestershire sauce, onion, sugar, poppy seeds and sesame seeds in a bowl and mix well. Add to the salad, tossing to coat well. Yields 10 to 12 servings.

The rural town of Exeter, established in 1742, is the site of the state's only continuously operated ski area. Yawgoo Valley Ski Area first opened in December of 1964. Offering 12 trails accessible by four different lifts, the area has day and evening skiing and snowboarding. With a winter sports season spanning the months from December to March, Yawgoo's natural snowfall is enhanced by 100 percent snow-making

Tomato Slices with Tabouli and Feta Vinaigrette

Serve this in the summer with grilled lamb or chicken or as a light first course.

~ 1 1/2 cups uncooked bulgur
~ 1 bunch scallions, minced
~ Leaves of 1 large bunch mint, minced
~ 1 English cucumber, seeded, minced
~ 1 small red onion, minced
~ Juice of 4 lemons
~ Grated zest of 2 lemons
~ 1/2 cup olive oil
~ Salt and pepper to taste
~ 3 (3-inch) beefsteak tomatoes
~ Feta Vinaigrette (below)

Soak the bulgur in lukewarm water to cover in a bowl for 15 minutes or longer. Drain and press in a cheesecloth to remove the moisture. Combine with the scallions, mint, cucumber and onion in a bowl. Add the lemon juice, lemon zest, olive oil, salt and pepper and mix well. Season to taste. Slice the tomatoes 3/4 inch thick. Fit into a 3-inch cookie cutter or juice can with a side 2 inches high. Pack the tabouli over the tomato slices in the cutter or can. Place on serving plates and gently remove. Drizzle with the Feta Vinaigrette. Garnish with sprigs of mint and additional lemon zest. Yields 6 to 8 servings.

Feta Vinaigrette

~ 1/4 cup extra-virgin olive oil
~ 2 tablespoons Dijon mustard
~ 1/4 cup red wine vinegar
~ 3/4 cup mineral water
~ 2 1/2 teaspoons lemon juice
~ 2 tablespoons chopped shallots
~ 1 tablespoon chopped fresh oregano
~ 1 tablespoon chopped fresh parsley
~ Salt and pepper to taste
~ 1/2 cup crumbled feta cheese

Whisk the olive oil gradually into the mustard in a medium bowl. Whisk in the vinegar, mineral water, lemon juice, shallots, oregano, parsley, salt and pepper. Add the cheese and whisk gently to mix well.
Yields 1 1/2 cups.

capabilities, and the facilities can accommodate up to 1,500 people a day. Hiking and mountain biking trails also are open to the public, as is a waterpark during the summer season.

Warm Spinach and Basil Salad

This goes well with almost everything. Try it with fresh pasta topped with a light tomato sauce.

- ~ 6 cups fresh spinach leaves
- ~ 2 cups fresh basil leaves
- ~ 3 cloves of garlic, minced
- ~ 1/2 cup pine nuts
- ~ 1/2 cup olive oil
- ~ 4 ounces prosciutto, chopped
- ~ Freshly ground pepper to taste
- ~ 3/4 cup grated Parmesan cheese

Toss the spinach and basil in a large salad bowl. Sauté the garlic and pine nuts in the heated olive oil in a medium skillet over medium heat until the pine nuts begin to brown slightly. Stir in the prosciutto. Cook for one minute longer. Season with pepper. Add to the spinach mixture and toss lightly. Sprinkle with the cheese. Serve immediately with additional freshly ground pepper. Yields 6 servings.

Fresh Watercress Salad

Serve watercress salad with turkey or pheasant and a Pinot Gris or a slightly sweet Riesling.

- ~ 2 tablespoons wine vinegar
- ~ Juice of 1/2 lemon
- ~ 1/4 cup olive oil
- ~ 1/4 cup vegetable oil
- ~ 2 tablespoons heavy cream
- ~ Salt to taste
- ~ 2 bunches watercress, stemmed
- ~ 1/2 cup crumbled bleu cheese
- ~ 2 Bosc pears, sliced
- ~ 1/2 cup toasted hazelnuts

Combine the vinegar, lemon juice, olive oil, vegetable oil, cream and salt in a bowl and mix well. Add the watercress and toss lightly. Top with the cheese, pears and hazelnuts. Yields 6 servings.

Fresh Herb Salad Dressing

Serve this easy dressing over a salad of mixed greens and top with hazelnuts, orange slices and/or red bell pepper strips.

- ~ 1/2 cup fresh orange juice
- ~ 2 tablespoons clover honey
- ~ 1 teaspoon minced fresh chervil

- ~ 1 teaspoon minced fresh chives
- ~ 1 teaspoon minced fresh tarragon
- ~ 1 teaspoon minced fresh parsley

- ~ Salt and white pepper to taste

Combine the orange juice, honey, chervil, chives, tarragon, parsley, salt and white pepper in a bowl. Whisk until smooth. Store in the refrigerator. Yields 4 servings.

Poppy Seed Salad Dressing

Serve this on a salad of spinach and oranges, watercress and water chestnuts or sliced fresh tomatoes.

- ~ 1 small onion, chopped
- ~ 2/3 cup raspberry vinegar

- ~ 2/3 cup sugar
- ~ 2 teaspoons dry mustard
- ~ Salt to taste

- ~ 2 cups corn oil
- ~ 3 tablespoons poppy seeds

Combine the onion with the vinegar, sugar, dry mustard and salt in a blender and process until chopped. Add the oil gradually and process until thickened and smooth. Combine with the poppy seeds in a bowl and mix well. Store in the refrigerator. Let stand until room temperature before serving. Yields 3 cups.

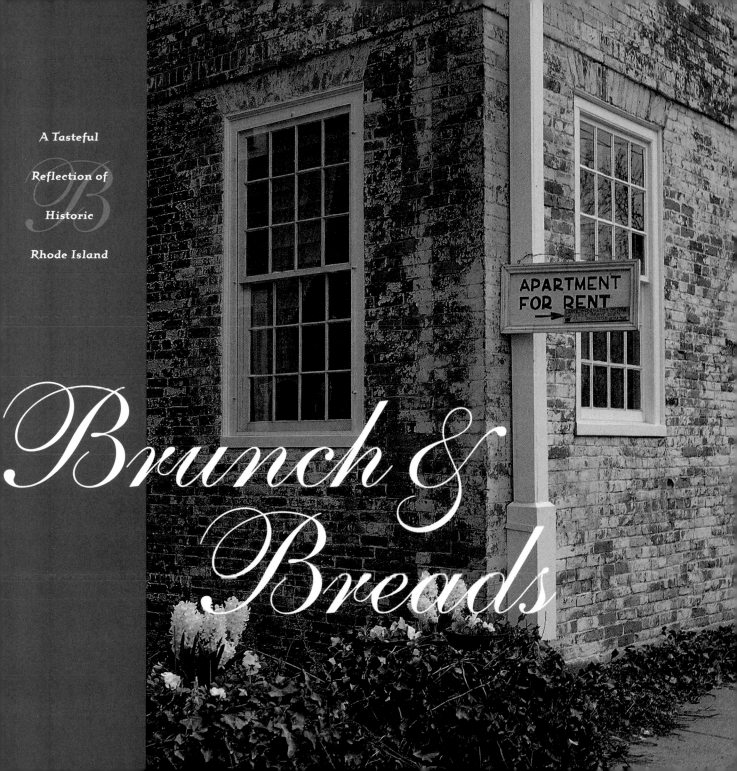

A Tasteful

Reflection of

Historic

Rhode Island

Brunch & Breads

Brunch

Cinnamon Apple Quiche, 67

Crunchy Fruit Dip, 65

Crustless Crab Quiche, 67

Elegant Pastry, 68

Elegant Quiche, 68

Fruit Dip, 65

Ham Pie, 69

Oven-Baked Western Frittata, 69

Sausage Squares with Artichokes and
    Spinach, 66

Southwestern Buffet Eggs, 70

Tomato and Chèvre Puffs, 66

Breads

All-Occasion Pancakes, 71

Apricot Cornmeal Muffins, 81

Baked Apple Pancakes, 71

Basic Biscuits, 70

Blueberry Lemon Brunch Cake, 77

Cardamom Sweet Rolls, 76

Cornmeal Pancakes with
    Maple-Cranberry Compote, 72

Cranberry-Almond Waffles, 75

Cranberry Bread, 79

Date Nut Bread, 79

Gingerbread with Cider Sabayon, 78

Johnnycakes, 72

Morning Glory Muffins, 82

New England Corn Cakes, 73

Overnight French Toast, 74

Popovers, 74

Quick Multi-Grain Bread, 80

Sausage Waffles with Potatoes and
    Apples, 75

Scrumptious Blueberry Muffins, 81

Zucchini Bread, 80

Brunch

Fruit Dip

Start your brunch with a selection of fresh fruit and this easy dip.

~ 16 ounces sour
  cream
~ 1/2 cup honey
~ 1/2 cup orange juice
~ 1 teaspoon pumpkin
  pie spice

Combine the sour cream, honey, orange juice and pumpkin pie spice in a bowl and mix well. Chill for 6 to 8 hours before serving. Yields 3 cups.

Crunchy Fruit Dip

The crushed cookies and walnuts give this dip a pleasing crunch.

~ 1/2 package crisp
  coconut cookies
~ 1 to 2 tablespoons
  brown sugar
~ 3 cups sour cream
~ 1/2 cup chopped
  walnuts (optional)
~ Assorted fresh fruit,
  such as melons,
  berries, tart apples
  or pineapple wedges

Crush the cookies with the brown sugar in a food processor. Combine with the sour cream and walnuts in a bowl and mix well. Serve with the fruit for dipping. Yields 5 cups.

In the early 19th century, Isaac Cundall and Jacob Babcock, two affluent town leaders in Ashaway, a village in rural Hopkinton, were actively involved in the temperance and anti-slavery movements. Babcock's Revolutionary War-era house was supposedly utilized as a stop on the Underground Railroad. The statewide political crusade to prohibit the sale, manufacture or imbibing of alcoholic

Sausage Squares with Artichokes and Spinach

This can be cut into smaller squares for a hearty appetizer.

~ 2 (6-ounce) jars marinated artichokes
~ 1 medium onion, chopped
~ 1 clove of garlic, minced

~ 1 (10-ounce) package frozen chopped spinach
~ 12 ounces sweet Italian sausage, crumbled
~ 5 eggs
~ 1/2 cup bread crumbs

~ 1/4 cup grated Parmesan cheese
~ 1/2 teaspoon oregano
~ Salt and pepper to taste
~ 2 cups shredded Cheddar cheese

Drain and chop the artichokes, reserving the marinade from one jar. Combine the marinade with the onion and garlic in a skillet. Sauté until the onion is tender. Cook the spinach using the package directions and drain well. Brown the sausage in a skillet; drain. Beat the eggs in a mixer bowl. Stir in the bread crumbs, Parmesan cheese, oregano, salt and pepper. Add the onion mixture, spinach, artichokes and sausage and mix well. Stir in the Cheddar cheese. Spoon into a 9x13-inch baking dish. Bake at 325 degrees for 30 minutes. Cut into squares and serve hot.
Yields 12 servings.

Tomato and Chèvre Puffs

This attractive accompaniment to a brunch or luncheon can also be served as a first course for a dinner or as an appetizer.

~ 1 sheet frozen puff pastry, thawed
~ 4 plum tomatoes, peeled, thinly sliced
~ 2 tablespoons chopped shallot

~ 8 ounces cream cheese
~ 2 ounces chèvre or other sharp goat cheese

~ 1 tablespoon anchovy paste
~ 1 tablespoon sour cream

Roll the puff pastry to 1 1/2 times its original size on a lightly floured surface. Cut into 2-inch circles. Place on a parchment-lined baking sheet. Bake at 400 degrees for 12 to 15 minutes or until puffed and golden brown. Top with the tomato slices. Process the remaining ingredients in a food processor until smooth. Spoon over the tomatoes. Broil for 2 to 3 minutes or just until light brown. Yields 8 servings.

**beverages was
supported so
strongly in the
Ashaway area that it
came to be called
"Temperance
Valley."**

Cinnamon Apple Quiche

Judy Rush of the International Gourmet Society, who contributed this recipe, serves it with a fresh fruit salad for a light brunch.

~ 7 ounces aged
  Vermont Cheddar
  cheese, shredded
~ 1 unbaked (10-inch)
  pie shell

~ 1 tart apple, peeled,
  shredded
~ 2 tablespoons butter
~ 1 1/2 cups heavy
  cream

~ 3 large eggs
~ 1 tablespoon sugar
~ 1/4 teaspoon
  cinnamon
~ Nutmeg to taste

Sprinkle the cheese in the pie shell. Sauté the apple in the butter in a small skillet for 5 minutes. Spread over the cheese. Process the cream, eggs, sugar and cinnamon in a blender until smooth. Pour over the apple layer and sprinkle with nutmeg. Bake at 375 degrees for 35 minutes or until the center is set and the top is golden brown.
Yields 6 to 8 servings.

Crustless Crab Quiche

You can easily serve six people with just six ounces of crab meat in this quiche which is actually not difficult to prepare.

~ 8 ounces fresh
  mushrooms,
  sliced
~ 2 tablespoons butter
  or margarine
~ 4 eggs
~ 1 cup sour cream

~ 1 cup small curd
  cottage cheese
~ 1 cup freshly grated
  Parmesan cheese
~ 1/4 cup flour
~ 4 drops of hot
  pepper sauce

~ 1 teaspoon onion
  powder
~ 1/4 teaspoon salt
~ 2 cups shredded
  Monterey Jack cheese
~ 6 ounces crab meat,
  drained

Sauté the mushrooms in the butter in a skillet until tender; drain. Combine the eggs, sour cream, cottage cheese, Parmesan cheese, flour, pepper sauce, onion powder and salt in a mixer bowl or blender and mix until smooth. Add the mushrooms, Monterey Jack cheese and crab meat and mix well. Pour into a coated 10-inch quiche pan. Bake at 350 degrees for 45 minutes or until a knife inserted near the center comes out clean. Let stand at room temperature for 5 minutes before serving.
Yields 6 servings.

The town of
North Providence,
separated from
Providence in 1765
on the principle of
religious toleration
and today has many
religious denomi-
nations represented
by its churches.
The May Breakfast,
a custom unique
to New England,
is practiced by many
churches and civic
groups. The custom,
which originated
in 1868, is a
celebration of
springtime and is
Rhode Island's
homage to the
ancient May
Day celebration

Elegant Quiche

Real men will eat quiche when you serve this elegant dish from Fran Babcock at the Sarah Kendall House Bed and Breakfast, Newport.

~ 1/2 cup finely
  minced shallots
~ 1/2 cup dry white
  wine
~ 6 eggs
~ 2 cups heavy cream

~ 1/4 teaspoon freshly
  grated nutmeg
~ 1 teaspoon salt
~ 1/4 teaspoon white
  pepper

~ 1/2 recipe Elegant
  Pastry (below)
~ 6 ounces Gruyère
  cheese

Bring the shallots to a boil in the wine in a small saucepan over low heat. Simmer for 2 minutes. Cool to room temperature. Combine the eggs and cream in a bowl and mix gently. Fold in the shallots, nutmeg, salt and white pepper. Roll the pastry dough into a circle on a floured surface. Fit into a 10-inch pie plate and trim and flute the edge. Sprinkle with the cheese. Add the egg mixture. Bake at 360 degrees for 45 minutes or until set. Yields 6 servings.

Elegant Pastry

This pastry can be used for all your pies and quiches: it comes out perfectly every time.

~ 2 1/2 cups flour
~ 1 teaspoon sugar
~ 1 teaspoon salt
~ 1/2 cup shortening

~ 1/2 cup unsalted
  butter, chilled, sliced
~ 1 1/2 teaspoons
  cider vinegar

~ 5 tablespoons
  (about) ice water

Combine the flour, sugar and salt in the food processor. Add the shortening and butter and process until the mixture resembles coarse cornmeal. Combine the vinegar and 2 tablespoons of the ice water in a small bowl. Add to the crumb mixture and mix well. Add the remaining water one tablespoon at a time, processing constantly until the mixture forms moist clumps which can be gathered into a soft dough. Divide into 2 portions, flatten into discs and wrap each in plastic wrap. Chill for 30 minutes. Yields 2 pastries.

practiced in Europe for centuries. It is usually held on the first day of May, when celebrants are served such favorites as baked ham, scrambled eggs, johnnycakes, home-fried potatoes, berry-filled muffins, baked beans, coffee, milk and apple cider.

Ham Pie

Featuring a variety of hams, this pie is perfect for an Easter brunch. It can also be prepared in a pastry-lined 9x12-inch baking dish.

~ 4 ounces baked ham or proscettini
~ 4 ounces Italian ham
~ 4 ounces Polish ham
~ 4 ounces cappicoli
~ 4 ounces salami

~ 1 pound Italian sausage, cooked
~ 4 ounces (scant) bacon, crisp-fried, crumbled
~ 3 hard-cooked eggs, chopped

~ 4 ounces fresh cheese or basket cheese, shredded
~ 2 tablespoons grated Parmesan cheese
~ 6 (about) eggs
~ Elegant Pastry (page 68)

Chop the ham, cold cuts, sausage and bacon into medium sized pieces by hand or in the food processor. Combine all the chopped meats in a bowl. Add the chopped eggs and cheese and mix gently. Add 3 eggs and mix well. Add remaining eggs one at a time, mixing until moistened to the desired consistency. Pour into two pie shells. Bake at 350 degrees for one hour or until the pies are set and the crusts are golden brown.
Yields 12 servings.

Oven-Baked Western Frittata

Serve this zesty omelet with muffins for a brunch or with soup and salad for lunch or supper.

~ 6 ounces Canadian bacon or sliced ham
~ 2 tablespoons vegetable oil

~ 3 green onions
~ 1 medium red bell pepper
~ 6 large eggs

~ 1 cup shredded Swiss cheese
~ 1/3 cup water
~ 1/4 teaspoon salt

Brown the Canadian bacon in half the oil in an ovenproof skillet; remove with a slotted spoon. Cut the green onions and bell pepper into 1/4-inch pieces. Sauté in the remaining oil in the skillet over medium-high heat for 5 minutes. Combine the eggs, cheese, water and salt in a bowl and mix well. Pour into the skillet. Sprinkle with the Canadian bacon. Bake at 375 degrees for 15 to 20 minutes or until set. You may stir the bacon into the egg mixture if you prefer. Yields 6 servings.

Biscuit City Road
runs through South
Kingstown. One of
the town's oldest
roads, in 1668 it
was called Zachary
Bridge Road. The
name change is
reportedly due to a
traveling salesman's
experience there.
Late one afternoon
he was making
door-to-door sales
calls in the area,
and at each house he
was greeted by a
woman with flour
on her hands who
said she had no
time to talk because
the oven was just

Southwestern Buffet Eggs

Judy Rush of the International Gourmet Society takes advantage of the growing taste for the Southwestern flavor with this easy brunch dish. Serve it with salsa and sour cream and add minced jalapeño peppers for a zippier taste.

~ 12 eggs
~ 2 (16-ounce) cans cream-style corn
~ 2 (4-ounce) cans chopped green chiles
~ 2 cups shredded extra-sharp Cheddar cheese
~ 2 cups shredded Monterey Jack cheese
~ Pepper to taste
~ 1 tablespoon instant grits
~ 1 1/2 teaspoons Worcestershire sauce

Beat the eggs in a mixing bowl. Add the corn, green chiles, shredded cheeses, pepper, grits, Worcestershire sauce and mix well. Spoon into a lightly greased 9x13-inch baking dish. Bake at 325 degrees for one hour or until the mixture is set and light brown on top. Yields 16 servings.

Basic Biscuits

Biscuit dough should be mixed gently to keep the biscuits light. For fluffier biscuits, place them close together on the baking sheet. For crustier biscuits, place them at least an inch apart.

~ 2 cups unbleached flour
~ 1 tablespoon baking powder
~ 1 teaspoon sugar
~ 1/2 teaspoon salt
~ 5 tablespoons unsalted butter, chilled, chopped
~ 3/4 cup half-and-half

Mix the flour, baking powder, sugar and salt in a large bowl. Cut in the butter with 2 knives or a pastry blender or mix with fingers until the mixture resembles coarse crumbs. Add the half-and-half and mix gently to form dough. Knead lightly on a floured surface for 30 seconds. Pat until 3/4 inch thick. Cut with a 2 3/4-inch cutter. Place one inch apart on a baking sheet. Bake at 450 degrees for 14 minutes or until puffed and golden brown. Yields 8 biscuits.

right for the supper biscuits. Discouraged, he took a room for the night in the Kingstown Inn. Asked where he had ended his work day, he replied, "Apparently Biscuit City." (Pettaquamscutt Historical Society)

Baked Apple Pancakes

Serve Baked Apple Pancakes hot with maple syrup or whipped cream.

~ 4 eggs, beaten
~ 1 cup milk
~ 1 cup flour
~ 1/4 teaspoon salt
~ 1/2 cup sugar

~ 1 tablespoon cinnamon
~ 3 medium apples, peeled, cut into 1/4-inch wedges

~ 1/4 cup butter, softened

Combine the eggs, milk, flour and salt in a bowl and whisk or beat with a rotary beater until smooth. Let stand for several minutes. Mix the sugar and cinnamon together. Sprinkle over the apples in a bowl and toss to mix well. Spread the butter in two 9-inch pie plates. Arrange the apples in the prepared plates. Spoon the batter evenly over the apples. Bake at 375 degrees for 30 to 40 minutes or until puffed, set and golden brown. Yields 8 servings.

All-Occasion Pancakes

Add lightly floured blueberries or sliced bananas or apples to this recipe before baking for a special treat. It would also be good with the Bourbon Peach Sauce (page 167) or Maple-Cranberry Compote (page 72).

~ 1 cup sifted flour
~ 2 teaspoons baking powder
~ 2 tablespoons sugar

~ Ginger, nutmeg, allspice and cinnamon to taste
~ 1/2 teaspoon salt

~ 1 cup milk
~ 3 tablespoons corn oil or canola oil
~ 1 egg

Sift the flour 2 times and remeasure, discarding any excess. Sift again with the baking powder, sugar, ginger, nutmeg, allspice, cinnamon and salt into a bowl. Add the milk, oil, and egg and mix just until moistened. Oil the griddle or skillet or spray with nonstick cooking spray. Heat until a few drops of water will skip on the surface. Ladle onto the griddle and bake for 2 minutes or until golden brown. Yields 3 or 4 servings.

Breads

Usquepaug is the location of the world-famous Kenyon Grist Mill. A versatile food, Rhode Island cornmeal is best known for its use in making johnnycakes. The Indians taught the area's earliest settlers to make these cakes. There is a statewide contro-versy regarding the proper preparation and spelling of jo(h)nnycakes. The West Bay or South County recipe involves scalding the meal and cooking

Johnnycakes

Serve this traditional New England treat with butter, maple syrup and sliced melon for a delightful brunch.

~ 2 cups white cornmeal
~ 2 teaspoons sugar
~ 1 1/2 teaspoons salt
~ 3 cups boiling water
~ 1/4 cup butter

Mix the cornmeal, sugar and salt in a large bowl. Stir in the boiling water; mixture will be stiff. Melt one tablespoon butter at a time on a large heavy griddle or skillet over medium heat. Drop the batter by tablespoonfuls into the butter, spreading into 2-inch circles. Cook for 4 minutes on each side or until golden brown. Repeat with the remaining batter, adding the remaining butter as needed.
Yields 46 small johnnycakes.

Cornmeal Pancakes with Maple-Cranberry Compote

The Maple-Cranberry Compote is delicious with these pancakes, but it could be served with a spiced hot mixture of any fruit in season.

~ 3/4 cup flour
~ 2 tablespoons sugar
~ 1/2 cup yellow cornmeal
~ 4 teaspoons baking powder
~ 3/4 teaspoon salt
~ 5 tablespoons unsalted butter
~ 1 cup milk
~ 2 large eggs, beaten
~ 1 cup fresh cranberries
~ 1 cup pure maple syrup

Mix the flour, sugar, cornmeal, baking powder and salt in a large bowl. Heat the butter in the milk in a small saucepan over low heat until the butter melts. Cool to lukewarm. Beat in the eggs. Add to the flour mixture and mix just until moistened. Heat a griddle until a few drops of water skip lightly on the surface and grease lightly. Spoon the batter into 5-inch rounds on the griddle. Bake for 2 minutes and turn. Bake for 1 minute longer. Wrap the cooked pancakes in a towel and hold in a warm oven until time to serve. Combine the cranberries with the maple syrup in a small saucepan. Cook over medium-low heat for 10 minutes or until the cranberries pop and the syrup turns red. Serve over the pancakes.
Yields 4 servings.

thick and crunchy cakes. East Bay or Newport County cakes are made with a milk batter and cooked thin and lacy-edged. Served with butter, maple syrup or gravy, either style is tasty.

New England Corn Cakes

These are a special treat from Jack and Marcia Felber at the Olympia Tea Room in Watch Hill, Rhode Island.

~ 2 cups unbleached flour
~ 2 cups cornmeal

~ 1/2 cup sugar
~ 1 teaspoon salt
~ 2 cups milk
~ 4 eggs

~ 1/2 cup melted butter
~ Maple Walnut Butter (below)

Sift the flour, cornmeal, sugar and salt into a bowl. Blend the milk, eggs and butter in a small bowl. Add to the dry ingredients and mix with a wooden spoon just until moistened. Spoon onto a griddle and bake until golden brown. Serve with Maple Walnut Butter. Yields 8 servings.

Maple Walnut Butter

~ 1/2 cup butter, softened
~ 1/2 cup pure maple syrup
~ 1/3 cup chopped walnuts

Combine the butter and maple syrup in a bowl and whip until smooth. Stir in the walnuts. Yields 1 1/3 cups.

Breads

Popovers

Bake popover batter in a muffin pan with a small amount of meat drippings to serve with beef or holiday poultry.

~ 1 cup flour
~ 1/2 teaspoon salt

~ 2 eggs
~ 1 cup milk

~ 1 tablespoon shortening

Sift the flour and salt together. Beat the eggs in a mixing bowl. Add the flour and 1/3 cup of the milk. Mix at low speed until moistened. Add the remaining milk and shortening and beat until smooth. Spoon into baking cups or muffin pan. Bake at 425 degrees for 40 minutes or until golden brown. Yields 6 servings.

Overnight French Toast

The beauty of this dish for hostess and guests alike is that it can be prepared in advance and everyone can be served at once.

~ 12 eggs or egg substitute to equal 12 eggs
~ 1/2 cup cream or low-fat milk

~ 2 tablespoons orange liqueur or orange juice
~ Grated zest of 1 orange

~ 1/2 teaspoon vanilla extract
~ 1 loaf French bread, sliced 1 inch thick

Combine the eggs, cream, liqueur, orange zest and vanilla in a shallow baking pan. Place the bread in the pan, turning to coat well. Cover the pan with a cover or plastic wrap and chill for 8 hours or longer. Remove the bread slices to a greased baking sheet. Bake at 375 degrees for 20 to 25 minutes or until golden brown. Serve with fruit, maple syrup or apple syrup. Yields 6 servings.

Sausage Waffles with Potatoes and Apples

Serve on warmed serving plates with warm syrup and a topping of additional chopped apples.

~ 6 ounces pork or turkey sausage
~ 1 1/2 cups flour
~ 1 1/2 teaspoons baking powder
~ 1/2 teaspoon baking soda
~ 1/4 teaspoon salt
~ 1 cup milk
~ 3 large egg yolks, at room temperature
~ 2 tablespoons melted butter
~ 1/2 cup chopped cooked potatoes
~ 1/2 cup grated peeled apple
~ 3 large egg whites, at room temperature

Cook the sausage in a skillet, stirring until crumbly; drain. Mix the flour, baking powder, baking soda and salt in a bowl. Combine the milk, egg yolks and butter in a small bowl and whisk until smooth. Add to the dry ingredients and stir just until moistened. Stir in the sausage, potatoes and apple. Beat the egg whites at high speed in a medium mixer bowl until stiff peaks form. Fold into the batter. Spoon into a preheated greased waffle iron. Bake using the manufacturer's instructions for 2 to 3 minutes or until golden brown. Place waffles directly on the rack in a 200-degree oven to keep warm. Yields 8 to 10 servings.

Cranberry-Almond Waffles

Cranberries are native to the bogs of New England and lend their tart taste to these easy waffles. Use frozen cranberries when the fresh ones are not available.

~ 1 egg
~ 3 tablespoons yellow cornmeal
~ 2 tablespoons bran
~ 1 tablespoon vegetable oil
~ 1 cup buttermilk
~ 1 cup buttermilk waffle mix
~ 1/4 cup (or more) water
~ 2 tablespoons chopped almonds or walnuts
~ 1/2 cup cranberries, cut into halves

Beat the egg in a mixing bowl. Add the cornmeal, bran, oil, buttermilk, waffle mix and water and mix well. Stir in the almonds and cranberries. Ladle onto a lightly oiled waffle iron and bake using the manufacturer's instructions. Yields 2 servings.

The history of
the island of
Jamestown,
strategically
situated at the
mouth of
Narragansett Bay,
involves many
stories of pirates,
privateers and
smuggling. The
island's Pirate's
Cave is thought to
contain the buried
treasure of Captain
Kidd, the infamous
British privateer-
turned-pirate who
is said to have
regularly evaded
British justice by
hiding in Rhode
Island waters. It is

Cardamom Sweet Rolls

The resulting taste treat will convince you that the time and trouble are worth it for these delicious rolls. You may frost them with a mixture of confectioners' sugar and orange juice if you prefer.

~ 1 1/4 ounces fresh
cake yeast
~ 8 1/2 ounces
lukewarm milk
~ 3 cups bread flour
~ 1/4 cup cake flour
~ 1/4 cup sugar
~ 1 egg

~ 1/4 cup unsalted
butter, softened
~ 1 1/8 teaspoon
ground cardamom
~ 1/2 teaspoon salt
~ 1 egg, beaten
~ 3/4 cup packed
brown sugar

~ 1/2 cup raisins
~ 3/4 teaspoon
cinnamon
~ 1 cup apricot jam
~ 1/4 cup sugar
~ 1 cup water

Dissolve the yeast in the milk in a large mixing bowl fitted with a dough hook. Add the bread flour, cake flour, sugar, one egg, butter, cardamom and salt. Mix at low speed for just 2 1/2 minutes. Place on a lightly floured surface, cover with plastic wrap and let rest for 10 minutes. Divide the dough into 2 portions and roll each portion into a rectangle 1/4 inch thick. Brush the surface with beaten egg, leaving a 1/2-inch edge. Sprinkle with the brown sugar, raisins and cinnamon. Roll the dough to enclose the filling; press the seams to seal. Slice into 1/2- to 3/4-inch slices. Place on a pachment-lined baking sheet. Cover with towels and let rise in a warm place until doubled in size. Bake at 375 degrees for 20 minutes or until golden brown. Bring the jam, sugar and water to a boil in a saucepan. Cook until the mixture coats the back of a spoon. Brush immediately over the rolls. Serve hot or cooled. Yields 12 servings.

known that he visited Jamestown sea captain Thomas Paine, who reportedly held some of Kidd's gold for him. Kidd's luck ran out in 1699, when he was captured and tried for murder and piracy. Despite his pleas of innocence, he was found guilty by a London court, and was hanged in 1701. British authorities never recovered his treasure.

(Watson 101)

Blueberry Lemon Brunch Cake

Serve this blueberry cake with the Spiced Blueberry Sauce for brunch, tea or dessert.

~ 1 cup blueberries
~ 1 tablespoon flour
~ 1/2 cup butter or margarine, softened
~ 1 cup sugar
~ 2 eggs
~ 1/2 cup milk
~ 1 2/3 cups flour
~ 1 1/2 teaspoons baking powder
~ 1/4 teaspoon salt
~ 1 tablespoon grated lemon rind
~ 1/4 cup sugar
~ 1/4 cup fresh lemon juice
~ Spiced Blueberry Sauce (below)

Toss the blueberries with 1 tablespoon flour in a bowl and set aside. Cream the butter and 1 cup sugar in a large mixing bowl until light and fluffy, scraping the bowl occasionally. Beat in the eggs 1 at a time. Add the milk, 1 2/3 cups flour, baking powder and salt and mix until smooth. Fold in the blueberries and lemon rind. Spoon into a greased and floured 5x9-inch loaf pan. Bake at 350 degrees for 60 to 70 minutes or until a wooden pick inserted into the center comes out clean. Cool in the pan on a wire rack for 10 minutes. Remove the cake to a serving plate and pierce with a wooden pick. Bring 1/4 cup sugar and lemon juice to a boil in a saucepan and cook until the sugar dissolves. Brush over the cake. Cool completely. Serve with the Spiced Blueberry Sauce. Yields 12 servings.

Spiced Blueberry Sauce

~ 1/4 cup sugar
~ 1/4 cup water
~ 2 cups fresh blueberries
~ 1/2 teaspoon cinnamon
~ 1/4 teaspoon nutmeg

Combine the sugar and water in a medium microwave-safe bowl. Microwave, covered, on High for 2 minutes. Crush one cup of the blueberries with a fork and add to the cooked syrup with the cinnamon and nutmeg. Microwave on High for 4 minutes. Stir in the remaining whole berries. Microwave for one minute longer. Cool slightly before serving. Yields 2 1/2 cups.

Hearthside, one of Rhode Island's finest Federal-era homes, is located on the Great Road in Lincoln. Built in 1810 by prominent Quaker and businessman Stephen H. Smith, the graceful fieldstone and granite mansion bears a sadly romantic folktale. Smith was enamored of a Providence debutante who wanted to marry a man of means. Smith purchased a Louisiana Lottery ticket and won his fortune. He

Gingerbread with Cider Sabayon

Welcome your family or guests with the delightful aroma and flavor of the essential comfort food. You can also scoop out some of the center of the gingerbread servings and fill with warm apples before you add the sabayon.

- ~ 1 1/2 cups boiling water
- ~ 1 cup molasses
- ~ 1 teaspoon baking soda
- ~ 1/2 cup unsalted butter, softened
- ~ 1 cup packed light brown sugar
- ~ 1 egg
- ~ 2 1/2 cups flour
- ~ 1 tablespoon baking powder
- ~ 2 teaspoons ginger
- ~ 1 1/4 teaspoons cinnamon
- ~ Pinch of ground cloves
- ~ 1/2 teaspoon salt
- ~ Cider Sabayon (below)

Bring the water to a boil in a small saucepan and stir in the molasses and baking soda; cool. Cream the butter and brown sugar with the paddle attachment in a mixing bowl for 2 minutes or until light. Mix in the egg. Sift the flour, baking powder, spices and salt together. Add to the creamed mixture alternately with the molasses mixture, mixing constantly at low speed. Spoon into a buttered 9x13-inch baking dish. Bake at 350 degrees for 30 to 35 minutes or until a tester comes out clean. Cool on a wire rack. Cut into 2x3-inch pieces and serve with Cider Sabayon.
Yields 18 servings.

Cider Sabayon

Apple juice and apple liqueur are substituted for the more traditional Marsala in this New England version of a French favorite.

- ~ 8 large egg yolks
- ~ 1/2 cup sugar
- ~ 1/2 cup plus 2 tablespoons apple juice
- ~ 2 tablespoons Calvados
- ~ 1 cup heavy cream

Combine the egg yolks and sugar in a large stainless steel bowl. Whisk in the apple juice and liqueur. Place over a saucepan of boiling water. Cook for 5 minutes or until the mixture has tripled in volume and is thickened, whisking constantly; the mixture should mound slightly. Place in a bowl with ice water 1/4 of the way up the side. Whisk until cold. Whip the cream at high speed in a mixer bowl until soft peaks form. Fold into the custard. Chill until serving time. Yields 5 cups.

then built this
elegant house
for his fiancée.
Unfortunately, the
lady spurned Smith
when she realized
how far she would
be living from the
sophistication
of Providence.
Smith remained
unmarried, living at
Hearthside with his
brother's family,
until his death.

Cranberry Bread

Cranberries have been referred to as bounceberries because the ripe ones bounce; it is still a good way to check for good ripe berries.

- ~ 2 cups flour
- ~ 1 1/2 teaspoons baking powder
- ~ 1/2 teaspoon baking soda
- ~ 1 cup sugar
- ~ Juice and grated rind of 1 orange
- ~ 2 tablespoons vegetable oil
- ~ Boiling water
- ~ 1 egg, beaten
- ~ 1 cup chopped walnuts (optional)
- ~ 1 cup fresh cranberries

Sift the flour, baking powder and baking soda into a bowl. Stir in the sugar. Combine the orange juice, orange rind, oil and enough boiling water to measure 3/4 cup in a measuring cup. Add the orange mixture and egg to the dry ingredients and mix well. Stir in the walnuts and cranberries. Spoon into a greased and floured 5x9-inch loaf pan. Bake at 325 degrees for 60 to 70 minutes or until a wooden pick comes out clean. Cool in the pan for several minutes; remove the bread to a wire rack to cool completely. Yields 1 loaf.

Date Nut Bread

This old-fashioned bread is a traditional holiday accompaniment to ham and turkey dinners. It will stay moist for up to two weeks.

- ~ 1 cup finely chopped dates
- ~ 3/4 cup chopped walnuts
- ~ 1 1/2 teaspoons baking soda
- ~ 3 to 8 tablespoons margarine
- ~ 1 cup boiling water
- ~ 2 eggs, beaten
- ~ 1 cup sugar
- ~ 1 1/2 cups flour
- ~ 1 teaspoon vanilla extract

Combine the dates, walnuts, baking soda, margarine and boiling water in a bowl and mix well. Let stand for several minutes. Combine the eggs and sugar in a mixing bowl and beat until thick and lemon-colored. Add the flour and vanilla and mix well. Stir in the date mixture. Spoon into a greased and floured loaf pan. Bake at 350 degrees for 50 minutes. Cool in the pan for several minutes and then remove the bread to a wire rack to cool completely. Yields 1 loaf.

The Towers of
of the Narragansett
Casino are the
surviving landmark
of the famous
Narragansett Pier
summer resort. In
the late 19th
century, wealthy and
aristocratic visitors
came to the resort to
vacation, attracted
by the luxurious
hotels, beautiful
beach and the
fashionable Casino.
Completed in 1886,
it housed stores,
dining rooms, cafes,
billiard parlors,
theaters, lounges
and lawn tennis.
Saturday evening
dances showcased

Quick Multi-Grain Bread

This is a delicious way to satisfy the dietary fiber requirements that we are so conscious of today.

~ 2 tablespoons cornmeal
~ 1 cup whole wheat flour
~ 1/2 cup rye flour
~ 1/2 cup oat bran
~ 1/2 cup cornmeal
~ 1 teaspoon baking soda
~ 1 teaspoon salt
~ 3 tablespoons vegetable oil
~ 1/4 cup molasses
~ 1/4 cup honey
~ 1 3/4 cups buttermilk
~ 1/4 cup sunflower seeds

Spray a loaf pan with nonstick cooking spray and sprinkle with 2 tablespoons cornmeal. Sift the whole wheat flour, rye flour, oat bran, 1/2 cup cornmeal, baking soda and salt into a bowl. Combine the oil, molasses, honey and buttermilk in a bowl and whisk until smooth. Add the dry ingredients gradually, mixing well after each addition. Spoon into the prepared pan and sprinkle with the sunflower seeds. Bake at 350 degrees for 1 hour or until the loaf tests done. Cool in the pan for 15 minutes; remove the bread to a wire rack to cool completely. Yields one loaf.

Zucchini Bread

Zucchini bread is especially good sliced one-half inch thick, lightly toasted and served with marmalade.

~ 3 large eggs
~ 1 cup vegetable oil
~ 2 cups sugar
~ 2 cups grated peeled zucchini
~ 2 teaspoons vanilla extract
~ 3 cups flour
~ 1/2 teaspoon baking powder
~ 1 teaspoon baking soda
~ 1 tablespoon cinnamon
~ 1/4 teaspoon allspice
~ 1/2 teaspoon salt
~ 1/2 cup chopped pecans (optional)

Beat the eggs in a mixing bowl until light and foamy. Add the oil, sugar, zucchini and vanilla and mix well. Mix the flour, baking powder, baking soda, cinnamon, allspice and salt together. Add to the zucchini mixture with the pecans and mix just until moistened. Spoon into two greased and floured 5x9-inch loaf pans. Bake at 325 degrees for one hour. Cool in the pans for several minutes; remove the bread to a wire rack to cool completely. Yields 2 loaves.

Breads

the country's finest orchestras. Fire destroyed most of the area hotels and the Casino in September of 1900. Rebuilt in 1910, the Towers are a reminder of the Pier's colorful past.

Apricot Cornmeal Muffins

These muffins are a little different and can be made with other jams of your choice for variety. They are especially attractive made in shell-shaped tins.

- ~ 1 cup yellow cornmeal
- ~ 1 cup flour
- ~ 1 tablespoon baking powder
- ~ 1 teaspoon salt
- ~ 1/3 cup apricot jam
- ~ 1/8 teaspoon orange oil
- ~ 2 large eggs, beaten
- ~ 3/4 cup milk
- ~ 1/4 cup melted butter

Sift the cornmeal, flour, baking powder and salt into a large bowl. Melt the jam with the orange oil in a small saucepan over medium heat; remove from the heat. Add the eggs and milk and mix well. Add to the dry ingredients with the butter and mix until smooth. Spoon into oiled muffin cups, filling nearly full. Bake at 425 degrees for 15 to 20 minutes or until golden brown. Reduce the heat to 400 degrees after 10 minutes if the muffins brown too quickly. Yields 16 muffins.

Scrumptious Blueberry Muffins

Hardy low-bush blueberries thrive in New England and lend their sweet flavor to many New England favorites. Rinse them only when ready to use and store in a moistureproof container in the refrigerator.

- ~ 3 1/2 cups sifted flour
- ~ 3/4 cup sugar
- ~ 2 tablespoons baking powder
- ~ 5 eggs, slightly beaten
- ~ 1/2 cup milk
- ~ 5 ounces unsalted butter, melted
- ~ 4 or 5 cups fresh or frozen blueberries
- ~ Sugar

Preheat the oven to 425 degrees. Mix the flour, 3/4 cup sugar and baking powder in a bowl. Add the eggs, milk and butter and mix just until moistened. Fold in the blueberries. Grease the tops of large muffin tins and line the cups with paper liners. Spoon the batter into the cups, filling to the top. Sprinkle generously with additional sugar. Reduce the oven temperature to 400 degrees. Bake the muffins on the middle oven rack for 25 minutes or until golden brown. Remove the muffins to a wire rack to cool. Yields 15 to 16 large muffins.

Morning Glory Muffins

Thanks to the Sconset Cafe on Nantucket Island for these muffins. Serve them with cream cheese and honey.

~ 2 1/4 cups flour
~ 1 1/4 cups sugar
~ 2 teaspoons baking soda
~ 1 tablespoon cinnamon
~ 1/2 teaspoon salt

~ 1/2 cup shredded coconut
~ 1/2 cup raisins
~ 2 cups grated carrots
~ 1 apple, shredded
~ 1 (8-ounce) can crushed pineapple, drained

~ 1/2 cup pecans or walnuts
~ 3 eggs
~ 1 cup vegetable oil
~ 1 teaspoon vanilla extract

Sift the flour, sugar, baking soda, cinnamon and salt into a large bowl. Add the coconut, raisins, carrots, apple, pineapple and pecans and mix well. Combine the eggs, oil and vanilla in a bowl and whisk until smooth. Add to the dry ingredients and mix well. Spoon into paper-lined muffin cups, filling to the top. Bake at 350 degrees for 30 to 35 minutes or until a wooden pick comes out clean. Cool in the pans for 10 minutes; remove the muffins to a wire rack to cool completely. Store for 24 hours before serving to develop the flavors. Yields 16 muffins.

A Tasteful

Reflection of

Historic

Rhode Island

Main Dishes

Meats

Barbecued Spareribs, 94

Beef Tips over Rice, 87

Butterflied Leg of Lamb, 91

Carbonnade de Boeuf à la
Flamande, 85

Crespelle di Vitello, 98

Filet Mignon with Roasted Peppers
and Olives, 86

Grilled Lamb Steaks with Dijon,
Mint Aïoli and Roasted Pine
Nuts, 92

Involtini di Vitello Tuscany, 101

Lamb Curry, 93

Lamb Chops with Mushroom Sauce, 93

Marinated London Broil, 87

Marinated Steak with Peppers and
Onions, 88

Oven Stew, 89

Pan-Seared Sirloin Steak in Red Wine
Sauce, 89

Pineapple Pork Roast, 95

Rabbit Stew with Capers, 101

Roast Pork, 97

Roast Herbed Leg of Lamb, 92

Roast Pork Loin with Grilled Tuscan
Polenta in a Whiskey-Pepper
Sauce, 96

Spicy Pepper Steak, 90

Stuffed Flank Steak in Red Wine
Sauce, 91

Unforgettable Lamb, 94

Veal in Basil and Dijon Sauce, 97

Veal Chops with Blackberries, 99

Veal Scallopini Alessio, 100

Veal Medallions in a Basil Crust with
Roasted Garlic Cream Sauce, 100

Veal Loin with Green Peppercorn
Sauce, 99

Poultry

Angel of Hearts, 102

Chicken Potpie, 111

Chicken Saltimbocca, 113

Chicken Twists, 113

Chicken with Dijon and Sherry
Sauce, 106

Chicken Marsala, 108

Chicken Chili, 106

Cornish Game Hens with Dijon Peach
Glaze, 114

Cranberried Chicken Breast, 105

Double-Crust Chicken and Cheese
Pie, 110

Garlic Chicken with Red Pepper, 107

Honey-Baked Chicken, 108

Lemon Chicken, 105

Mexican Chicken Torte, 109

Roasted Chicken with Mustard and
Honey Glaze, 103

Sabra Chicken, 104

Southwestern Chicken Potpie, 112

Carbonnade de Boeuf à la Flamande

The molasses substitutes for the brown sugar which is usually found with beer, bacon and onions in this hearty Belgian beef stew from Flanders. The addition of 1 1/2 cups sour cream turns it into a delicious Stroganoff.

- ~ 3 pounds beef chuck or rump, cubed
- ~ 2 tablespoons butter
- ~ 2 tablespoons bacon drippings or vegetable oil
- ~ 1 1/2 pounds yellow onions, thinly sliced
- ~ Pinch of sugar
- ~ 2 cloves of garlic, crushed
- ~ Salt and pepper to taste
- ~ 1 bay leaf
- ~ 1 teaspoon thyme
- ~ 1 tablespoon chopped parsley
- ~ 1 1/2 tablespoons molasses
- ~ 1 (12-ounce) bottle beer
- ~ 1 cup beef stock
- ~ 2 cups sliced baby carrots
- ~ 2 tablespoons sugar
- ~ 3/4 cup chopped potatoes (optional)
- ~ 3/4 cup sliced mushrooms (optional)

Brown the beef in the heated butter and bacon drippings in a skillet, removing the beef with a slotted spoon. Reduce the heat and add the onions; sprinkle with a pinch of sugar. Sauté until transparent. Stir in the garlic, salt and pepper. Layer the beef and onions in a heavy baking dish or Dutch oven. Add the bay leaf and sprinkle with the thyme and parsley. Add the molasses, beer and beef stock. Bake, covered, at 350 degrees for 2 1/2 hours or until done to taste. Cook the carrots with 2 tablespoons sugar in water in a saucepan until tender; drain. Cook the potatoes in water in a saucepan until tender. Sauté the mushrooms in a nonstick skillet. Add the carrots, potatoes and mushrooms to the meat mixture and mix gently; discard the bay leaf. Yields 8 servings.

Main Dishes

Filet Mignon with Roasted Peppers and Olives

The roasted peppers, kalamata olives and tangy-sweet balsamic vinegar mingle to form a sauce that is assertive as well as colorful.

- ~ 1 red bell pepper
- ~ 1 yellow bell pepper
- ~ 2 (8- to 9-ounce) filet mignon steaks
- ~ Salt and pepper to taste
- ~ 1 1/2 tablespoons vegetable oil
- ~ 3 large cloves of garlic, minced
- ~ 2/3 cup reduced-sodium chicken broth
- ~ 1/3 cup pitted kalamata olives
- ~ 2 teaspoons balsamic vinegar or red wine vinegar
- ~ 1 tablespoon minced fresh oregano or 1 teaspoon dried oregano
- ~ 2 tablespoons unsalted butter

Roast the bell peppers over a gas flame or under the broiler until blackened on all sides. Place in a paper bag and let stand for 15 minutes. Peel, stem and seed the peppers; cut into thin strips. Season the steaks with salt and pepper. Brown in the heated oil in a large heavy skillet for 4 minutes on each side for rare. Remove to heated plates and keep warm with a foil cover. Add the bell peppers and garlic to the same skillet. Cook for 30 seconds. Add the chicken broth, olives, vinegar and oregano. Cook for 8 minutes or until the liquid is reduced to a glaze, stirring to deglaze the skillet; remove from the heat. Whisk in the butter. Season with salt and pepper. Spoon sauce over and around the beef to serve.

Yields 2 servings.

Beef Tips over Rice

Serve with fresh bread, a tossed salad and a Gristina Vineyards Merlot.

~ 2 pounds lean stew beef, cut into 1-inch cubes
~ 2 tablespoons shortening
~ 1 (10-ounce) can beef consommé
~ 1/3 cup cranberry juice
~ 2 tablespoons soy sauce
~ 2 teaspoons garlic juice
~ 1/2 teaspoon onion salt (optional)
~ 2 tablespoons cornstarch
~ 1/4 cup water
~ 4 cups cooked rice

Brown the beef on all sides in the shortening in a skillet. Stir in the beef consommé, cranberry juice, soy sauce, garlic juice and onion salt. Bring to a boil and reduce the heat. Simmer, covered, for 1 1/2 hours. Blend the cornstarch and water in a cup. Add to the skillet. Bring to a boil, stirring constantly. Cook for one minute longer or until thickened, stirring constantly. Serve over the rice. Yields 4 servings.

Marinated London Broil

The marinade will tenderize and add moisture to a cut of beef that is very lean and can be dry if not prepared correctly.

~ 1 cup beer
~ 1/4 cup soy sauce
~ 1/4 cup orange juice
~ 2 tablespoons vinegar
~ 1/2 small onion, chopped
~ 2 cloves of garlic, crushed
~ 2 tablespoons brown sugar
~ 1/4 teaspoon ginger
~ 1 (3-pound) London broil

Combine the beer, soy sauce, orange juice, vinegar, onion, garlic, brown sugar and ginger in a shallow dish and mix well. Add the beef and coat well. Marinate in the refrigerator for several hours; drain. Grill the beef until done to taste. Yields 8 servings.

Main Dishes

North Kingstown's village of Wickford, a historic seaport, was the site of an election supper given for President Andrew Jackson's supporters during the presidential campaign of 1832. The collation, or feast, "was more than usual in its conviviality and hilarity with plenty of wet goods dispensed." A nearby crossroads, regularly used as a lunch stop by farmers herding their cattle to market, has been known as Collation Corners ever since.

(Simister 49)

Marinated Steak with Peppers and Onions

This is delicious served with Baked Cheese Potatoes (page 144).

~ 8 large cloves of garlic, minced
~ 1/2 cup soy sauce
~ 1/4 cup balsamic vinegar or red wine vinegar
~ 1/2 cup olive oil
~ 4 teaspoons dried rosemary, crushed
~ 1 (3 1/2-pound) boneless top sirloin steak, 2 inches thick
~ Pepper to taste
~ Peppers and Onions (below)

Combine the garlic, soy sauce, vinegar, olive oil and rosemary in a bowl and mix well. Add the steak, turning to coat well. Season with pepper. Marinate, covered, in the refrigerator for 8 hours or longer. Let stand until room temperature. Drain, reserving the marinade. Place the steak in a broiler pan. Broil for 10 minutes on each side or to 125 degrees on a meat thermometer for rare. Place on a platter and let stand for 10 minutes. Slice the steak thinly across the grain and arrange the slices on a platter. Spoon the Peppers and Onions around the steak. Heat the reserved marinade in a saucepan. Serve with the steak. Yields 6 servings.

Peppers and Onions

~ 2 large onions, coarsely chopped
~ 1/3 cup olive oil
~ 2 red bell peppers, coarsely chopped
~ 1 green bell pepper, coarsely chopped
~ 3/4 teaspoon dried marjoram, crushed
~ 1/8 teaspoon crushed red pepper
~ Salt and pepper to taste

Sauté the onions in the heated olive oil in a large heavy skillet for 4 minutes. Add the bell peppers and sauté for 8 minutes or just until tender. Stir in the marjoram, red pepper, salt and pepper. Cook for 2 minutes longer. Yields 6 servings.

Oven Stew

Add the vegetables that suit your taste to this versatile recipe. You may also increase the tomatoes until the stew is of the consistency you prefer. Serve it with a Sakonnet Vineyards Rhode Island Red.

~ 2 (15-ounce) cans tomatoes
~ 3 tablespoons uncooked quick-cooking tapioca
~ 1 tablespoon sugar
~ 2 tablespoons dried basil
~ Salt and pepper to taste
~ 2 pounds cubed stew beef
~ 1 onion, chopped
~ 3 carrots, peeled, cut into 1-inch pieces
~ 3 potatoes, peeled, cut into 1-inch pieces
~ 2 stalks celery, cut into 1-inch pieces

Combine the undrained tomatoes, tapioca, sugar, basil, salt and pepper in a large Dutch oven and mix well. Add the beef, onion, carrots, potatoes and celery and mix. Bake, covered, at 350 degrees for 2 1/2 hours or until the beef is tender, stirring occasionally. Yields 4 to 6 servings.

Pan-Seared Sirloin Steak in Red Wine Sauce

This is an excellent choice for a last-minute company meal, elegantly served with fresh garden vegetables and buttered new potatoes.

~ 1 cup chopped green onions with tops
~ 2 tablespoons chopped shallots
~ 1/2 bay leaf, crumbled
~ 1 teaspoon minced fresh thyme
~ 2 tablespoons butter
~ 1 1/2 cups dry red wine
~ 1 (3 1/2-pound) boneless sirloin steak, 1 1/2 inches thick
~ 3 tablespoons minced parsley
~ 1 tablespoon fresh lemon juice
~ 1 tablespoon flour
~ 2 tablespoons butter

Saute the green onions and shallots with the bay leaf and thyme in 2 tablespoons melted butter in a skillet for 2 to 3 minutes or until the green onions are tender. Add the wine. Cook until reduced by 1/3. Spoon into a bowl and reserve. Sear the steak for 1 1/2 minutes on each side in the same skillet over high heat. Reduce the heat to medium and cool the skillet slightly. Stir in the reserved sauce, parsley, lemon juice, flour and 2 tablespoons butter. Cook for 2 to 4 minutes on each side or until done to taste. Cut the steak diagonally into 2-inch strips; serve with the sauce. Yields 6 servings.

Spicy Pepper Steak

Enjoy a Ridge Zinfandel, 1992, or a Chapoutier Crozes Hermitage, 1993 with this dish.

- ~ 1/2 cup soy sauce
- ~ 1/3 cup olive oil
- ~ 1 clove of garlic, minced
- ~ 1 teaspoon paprika
- ~ 1/2 teaspoon ground ginger
- ~ 1 1/2 pounds beef, cut into strips

- ~ 1 1/2 cups sliced red, yellow and green bell peppers
- ~ 1 cup thinly sliced celery
- ~ 1 cup sliced green onions
- ~ 1 tablespoon cornstarch

- ~ 3/4 cup water
- ~ 1 cup chopped fresh tomatoes
- ~ Salt and pepper to taste

Combine the soy sauce, 1/4 cup of the olive oil, garlic, paprika and ginger in a shallow dish. Add the beef and toss to coat well. Marinate at room temperature for 30 minutes or longer; drain. Sauté in the remaining olive oil in a large heavy skillet or wok over high heat until evenly browned. Add a small amount of water and simmer over medium heat for up to 20 minutes if needed to tenderize. Remove with a slotted spoon. Add the bell peppers, celery and green onions to the skillet. Sauté over medium-high heat for 10 minutes or until tender-crisp. Add the beef. Blend the cornstarch into the water in a cup. Stir into the skillet. Cook until thickened, stirring constantly. Stir in the tomatoes, salt and pepper and cook until heated through. Yields 4 servings.

Stuffed Flank Steak in Red Wine Sauce

A Chamard Vineyards Merlot or a Palmer Vineyards Cabernet Sauvignon goes well with this dish, which is best cooked medium-rare. Make enough to have leftovers: they are just as good as the first day.

~ 1/2 (10-ounce) package frozen chopped broccoli, thawed
~ 2 1/2 ounces garlic-herb cheese

~ 1 (1 1/4-pound) flank steak, trimmed
~ Salt and pepper to taste
~ 1 tablespoon vegetable oil

~ 1/2 cup beef broth
~ 1/3 cup dry red wine
~ 1 1/4 teaspoons flour
~ 1 teaspoon butter or margarine, softened

Press the broccoli to remove excess moisture. Combine with the cheese in a bowl and mix well with a fork. Sprinkle the steak with salt and pepper. Spread with the broccoli mixture, leaving a one-inch edge. Roll the meat to enclose the filling and tuck the ends under, securing with a wooden pick. Brown in the heated oil in a deep 10-inch skillet over high heat for 5 minutes. Drain the skillet and stir in the beef broth and wine. Simmer, covered, over low heat for 18 minutes for medium-rare or to 140 degrees on a meat thermometer. Remove the steak to a serving platter. Blend the flour with the butter in a small bowl. Stir into the pan juices. Cook over medium heat for 2 minutes or until thickened, whisking constantly. Cut the steak into 1/2-inch slices; serve with the sauce. Yields 4 servings.

Butterflied Leg of Lamb

Double the sauce ingredients if you like more to pass with the lamb.

~ 2 tablespoons soy sauce
~ 2 tablespoons olive oil

~ 1/2 teaspoon ground ginger
~ 2 cloves of garlic, crushed

~ 1/2 cup Dijon mustard
~ 1 leg of lamb, butterflied

Mix the soy sauce, olive oil, ginger, garlic and mustard in a bowl. Rub on the lamb in a shallow dish. Marinate in the refrigerator for several hours, turning occasionally. Drain the marinade into a saucepan. Place the lamb in a broiler pan. Broil for 15 minutes on each side. Bake at 350 degrees for 30 minutes or until done to taste. Heat the reserved marinade until bubbly. Serve with the lamb. Yields 6 to 8 servings.

Main Dishes

Slater Mill, built in 1790 on the banks of the Blackstone River in Pawtucket, is the site of the first successful water-powered, cotton-spinning machine in America. The opening of this mill marked the birth of the American Industrial Revolution and the transformation of America into an industrial society. The mill was built based on the machinery designs of famed English inventor Richard Arkwright. The

Roast Herbed Leg of Lamb

This is a great dish to serve at Easter. Serve it with gravy made with drippings from the roasting pan.

~ 1 cup white wine
~ 1/2 cup water
~ 1 cup olive oil
~ 1 tablespoon lemon juice
~ 1 onion, chopped

~ 2 cloves of garlic
~ 1 1/2 teaspoons salt
~ 1 teaspoon tarragon vinegar
~ 1 teaspoon crushed marjoram

~ 1 teaspoon crushed rosemary
~ 8 whole peppercorns, crushed
~ 1 (4- to 6-pound) leg of lamb

Combine the wine, water, olive oil, lemon juice and onion in a shallow dish. Mash the garlic with the salt and add to the marinade. Stir in the vinegar, marjoram, rosemary and peppercorns. Add the lamb and turn to coat well. Marinate in the refrigerator for 8 hours or longer, turning occasionally. Drain, reserving the marinade. Place the lamb on a rack in a roasting pan. Roast at 325 degrees for 2 to 2 1/2 hours or to 170 to 180 degrees on a meat thermometer, basting occasionally with the reserved marinade. Remove to a heated platter. Let stand for 10 to 15 minutes before carving. Yields 8 to 10 servings.

Grilled Lamb Steaks with Dijon, Mint Aïoli and Roasted Pine Nuts

Providence's Rue de l'espoir Restaurant, located on Hope Street, literally translates as "Street of Hope." Enjoy this dish with a Chateau Greysac, 1990, or a Kendall Jackson Merlot, 1992.

~ 5 egg yolks
~ 3 cups olive oil
~ 5 cloves of garlic, minced
~ 1/2 cup Dijon mustard

~ 1/2 cup lemon juice
~ Mint to taste
~ Salt to taste
~ Cayenne pepper and black pepper to taste

~ 1/2 cup roasted pine nuts
~ 8 (8-ounce) lamb steaks

Process the egg yolks in the food processor until smooth. Add the olive oil very gradually, processing constantly until thick. Combine with next 8 ingredients. Grill the lamb steaks until done to taste. Serve with the aïoli. Yields 8 servings.

popular lore is that Samuel Slater, an immigrant from Great Britain, memorized these designs while working on Arkwright machines during his apprenticeship in England, and then replicated them here in America.

Lamb Chops with Mushroom Sauce

The sauce that goes with this easy dish is especially good over noodles.

~ 6 lamb chops
~ 2 tablespoons olive oil
~ 8 ounces fresh mushrooms, sliced
~ 1 large onion, sliced
~ 1/2 cup stock, wine or water
~ 1/2 teaspoon rosemary
~ 1 clove of garlic, crushed
~ Salt and pepper to taste

Brown the chops quickly in the heated olive oil in a skillet. Remove the chops to a baking dish. Sauté the mushrooms and onions in the drippings in the skillet, adding additional oil if needed. Stir in the stock, rosemary, garlic, salt and pepper. Pour over the lamb. Bake, covered, at 350 degrees for 20 minutes. *Yields 3 servings.*

Lamb Curry

This is delicious served with bowls of chopped green pepper, pineapple chunks, chutney, raisins or peanuts. The flavor actually improves with reheating on the second day. Serve it with a Havens Syrah, 1990, or a Ravenswood Zinfandel, 1992.

~ 2 tablespoons chopped onion
~ 2 tablespoons butter
~ 2 tablespoons flour
~ 1 teaspoon curry powder
~ 2 cups chicken bouillon
~ 1 teaspoon lemon juice (optional)
~ 2 cups cubed cooked lamb
~ Salt and freshly ground pepper to taste
~ Cooked rice
~ Toppings such as chopped green pepper, pineapple chunks, chutney, raisins or coarsely chopped peanuts

Sauté the onion in the butter in a saucepan. Stir in the flour and curry powder. Add the bouillon and lemon juice. Cook over low to medium heat until slightly thickened, stirring constantly. Add the lamb. Cook until heated through. Season with salt and pepper. Serve over cooked rice with the toppings of your choice. *Yields 6 to 8 servings.*

Main Dishes

Oak Glen, an 1870s
Victorian house on
Union Street in
Portsmouth, was the
summer home of
Julia Ward Howe,
an extraordinary
reformer and writer
who was the first
woman member of
the American
Academy of Arts
and Letters. She is
best remembered for
her composition
"Battle Hymn of
the Republic," the
Union Army anthem
during the Civil
War. Howe, along
with her philan-
thropist husband,
Samuel Gridley
Howe, entertained

Unforgettable Lamb

This easy dish can be made in advance for a care-free dinner. Serve
it with a Wine Havens Merlot, 1992, or a Chateau de Clairefont
(Margaux), 1990.

~ 1 large eggplant,
sliced
~ Olive oil
~ 2 pounds lamb,
cubed

~ 1 large can tomatoes
with liquid, coarsely
chopped
~ 1 cup (or more)
crumbled feta cheese

~ 2 cloves of garlic,
minced (optional)
~ 1 can pitted black
olives, drained

Layer the eggplant in a small amount of olive oil in a large baking pan.
Bake at 350 degrees until nearly cooked through, turning once. Layer
the cooked eggplant, lamb, tomatoes, cheese, garlic and olives in a baking
dish. Bake, covered, at 350 degrees for 45 minutes. Bake, uncovered, for
30 minutes longer. Yields 6 servings.

Barbecued Spareribs

Serve Citrus Coleslaw (page 55) with this traditional favorite.

~ 3 to 4 pounds
spareribs or
trimmed country
ribs
~ Juice of 1 lemon
~ 6 tablespoons
vinegar
~ 1 cup catsup

~ 2 tablespoons
Worcestershire
sauce
~ 2 teaspoons
prepared mustard
~ 2 cups canned peeled
tomatoes

~ 1/4 cup chopped
onion
~ 1/4 cup packed
brown sugar
~ 1 tablespoon salt
~ 1/4 teaspoon pepper

Brown the ribs on all sides in a large skillet. Remove to a baking dish.
Combine the lemon juice, vinegar, catsup, Worcestershire sauce,
mustard, tomatoes, onion, brown sugar, salt and pepper in a bowl
and mix well. Pour over the spareribs. Bake, covered, at 350 degrees
for 1 1/4 hours, basting occasionally. Bake, uncovered, for 15 minutes
longer. Yields 6 servings.

Main Dishes

such guests as Henry
W. Longfellow,
Oscar Wilde and
Ralph Waldo
Emerson at Oak
Glen between 1870
and 1910.

Pineapple Pork Roast

The pineapple and apricot give a flavor of the islands to this pork roast.

~ 1 small onion, sliced
~ 1/4 cup chopped celery
~ 1/4 cup chopped carrots

~ 1 (3-pound) rolled and tied boneless pork loin roast
~ Salt and pepper to taste
~ 1 small bay leaf, crumbled

~ 1/2 cup pineapple juice
~ 1/4 cup soy sauce
~ 1 teaspoon cornstarch
~ 1/4 cup apricot jam

Sprinkle the onion, celery and carrots in a greased roasting pan. Season the roast with salt and pepper and place fat side on the vegetables; sprinkle with the bay leaf. Insert a meat thermometer horizontally into one end of the roast. Roast at 325 degrees for 45 minutes or until brown. Turn roast and bake for 30 minutes longer to brown bottom. Turn roast again and strain pan drippings. Pour a mixture of the pineapple juice and soy sauce over the roast. Roast for 15 to 25 minutes longer or to 170 degrees on the meat thermometer. Remove the roast to a platter and strain the pan juices. Sprinkle the vegetables over the roast. Stir the cornstarch into the apricot jam in a cup. Stir into the pan juices in a saucepan. Cook over medium heat until slightly thickened, stirring constantly. Spoon some of the glaze over the roast. Let stand for 10 minutes. Slice the roast and spoon the remaining glaze over the slices. Yields 10 servings.

Roast Pork Loin with Grilled Tuscan Polenta in a Whiskey-Pepper Sauce

The flavor of Italy comes to us with this recipe from Fabrizio Iannucci of Il Piccolo and Pizzico Restaurants. He recommends a Banfi Brunello di Montalcino, 1988, from Tuscany.

- ~ 1 (3-pound) pork loin roast
- ~ 3 ounces olive oil
- ~ Salt and pepper to taste
- ~ 2 cloves of garlic
- ~ 1 sprig of rosemary
- ~ 1 sprig of thyme, chopped
- ~ 4 ounces white wine
- ~ 2 ounces Irish whiskey
- ~ 2 ounces cracked black peppercorns
- ~ Grilled Tuscan Polenta (below)

Brush the pork with the olive oil and sprinkle with salt and pepper. Place in a 16-inch roasting pan and add the garlic, rosemary and thyme. Roast at 375 degrees for 45 minutes. Add the wine and roast to 155 degrees on a meat thermometer. Remove the roast to a serving platter, reserving the drippings. Combine the drippings with the whiskey and peppercorns in a saucepan. Simmer until reduced by 1/2. Serve the pork and sauce with Grilled Tuscan Polenta. Yields 3 to 4 servings.

Grilled Tuscan Polenta

- ~ 1 quart water
- ~ 3 ounces butter
- ~ Salt and pepper to taste
- ~ 6 to 8 ounces coarsely ground yellow cornmeal
- ~ 4 ounces bacon, chopped
- ~ 1 small yellow onion, coarsely chopped
- ~ 4 ounces cooked cannellini beans
- ~ 1 sprig of rosemary, chopped
- ~ 2 ounces Parmesan cheese, grated

Bring the water, butter, salt and pepper to a boil in a large saucepan. Stir in the cornmeal gradually. Cook for 15 minutes or until thickened, stirring constantly. Cook the bacon with the onion in a sauté pan until golden brown. Add to the cornmeal mixture with the beans and rosemary. Pour onto an oiled wooden or marble surface. Sprinkle with the cheese and smooth to 1/2-inch thickness. Cool and cut as desired. Grill on a hot griddle. Yields 3 to 4 servings.

Roast Pork

Wild Rice with Pecans (page 154) is good with this dish. Add a Chateau de la Chaize Brouilly, 1993, or a Ferrari Carano Merlot, 1991.

- ~ 1/2 cup dry white wine
- ~ 1/4 cup vegetable oil
- ~ 6 tablespoons Dijon mustard
- ~ 2 tablespoons soy sauce

- ~ 2 tablespoons fresh lemon juice
- ~ 2 tablespoons melted butter
- ~ 2 tablespoons minced onion
- ~ 1/4 cup (or more) chopped mushrooms

- ~ 1/2 teaspoon salt
- ~ 1/2 teaspoon celery seeds
- ~ 1/4 teaspoon freshly ground pepper
- ~ 1 (5-pound) rolled and tied boneless pork loin roast

Combine the wine, oil, mustard, soy sauce, lemon juice, butter, onion, mushrooms, salt, celery seeds and pepper in a shallow bowl and mix well. Add the pork roast. Marinate, covered, for 24 hours, turning occasionally. Drain, reserving the marinade. Place the pork in a roasting pan. Roast at 350 degrees for 2 1/2 hours or to 155 to 160 degrees on a meat thermometer, basting frequently with the reserved marinade during the last 30 minutes. Yields 8 to 10 servings.

Veal in Basil and Dijon Sauce

Complete this meal with steamed green beans and Lemon and Chive Potatoes (page 145) or Risotto with Asparagus and Pine Nuts (page 151). Add a Jordan Cabernet, 1991, or a Monsanto Chianti Clasic Riserva, 1990.

- ~ 8 ounces veal scallopini
- ~ Salt and freshly ground pepper to taste
- ~ Flour

- ~ 1/4 cup olive oil
- ~ 1 tablespoon minced shallots
- ~ 1/2 cup marsala wine
- ~ 2 tablespoons Dijon mustard

- ~ 1/4 cup chopped fresh basil
- ~ 2 tablespoons unsalted butter

Pound the veal 1/4 inch thick and season with salt and pepper. Coat with flour. Sauté in the heated olive oil in a skillet over medium-high heat for 2 minutes on each side. Remove to a warm platter. Cook the shallots in the drippings in the skillet. Add the wine, stirring to deglaze the skillet. Cook until reduced by 1/2. Stir in the mustard and basil. Remove from the heat. Whisk in the butter. Serve with the veal. Yields 2 servings.

West Warwick, set apart from Warwick as a separate town in 1913, is a series of mill villages running along the Pawtuxet River. The Lippitt Mill, built in 1809 by Revolutionary War Colonel Christopher Lippitt, is one of Rhode Island's most important examples of early industrial architecture and may be the oldest American textile mill still in operation. The Lippitt family, like the Spragues of Cranston, created a

Crespelle di Vitello

You will get enthusiastic reviews for these baby crepes stuffed with roasted veal and fresh herbs created by Capriccio Restaurant.

~ 4 eggs, beaten
~ 1 1/2 cups sifted flour
~ 2 cups milk
~ 2 pounds lean veal
~ 1 medium carrot, chopped
~ 1/2 medium yellow onion, chopped
~ 1 stalk celery, chopped

~ 2 shallots, chopped
~ 3 cloves of garlic
~ 2 sprigs of thyme
~ 2 sprigs of rosemary
~ 6 sage leaves
~ 1 bay leaf
~ Salt to taste
~ 1/4 teaspoon ground peppercorns
~ 1 cup dry white wine
~ 2 eggs

~ 1 cup grated Parmesan cheese
~ 10 sprigs chopped Italian parsley
~ Basil and Tomato Sauce (below)
~ Grated Parmesan cheese

Beat the eggs and flour in a bowl. Add the milk gradually, mixing until smooth. Spoon a small amount at a time into a heated crepe pan, swirling to coat well. Bake until golden brown. Combine the next 12 ingredients in a bowl and mix well. Spoon into a baking dish brushed with olive oil. Bake at 400 degrees for 20 minutes. Stir in the wine. Bake for 10 minutes longer. Grind until finely ground. Cool for 15 minutes. Mix with the eggs, 1 cup cheese and parsley in a bowl. Spoon onto the crepes and fold over like an envelope to enclose the filling. Arrange in a greased baking dish. Spoon the Basil and Tomato Sauce over the top and sprinkle with additional cheese. Bake for 15 minutes or until golden brown. Yields 6 servings.

Basil and Tomato Sauce

~ 1 shallot, chopped
~ 1 clove of garlic, chopped
~ 2 ounces olive oil
~ Oregano to taste

~ 1 (16-ounce) can peeled Italian tomatoes, crushed
~ Salt and pepper to taste

~ 2 ounces grappa
~ 3 ounces heavy cream
~ 1/4 cup butter
~ 8 basil leaves

Sauté the shallot and garlic in the oil in a large saucepan. Add the oregano, tomatoes, salt and pepper. Simmer for 10 minutes. Add the grappa and cream. Cook for 5 minutes. Stir in the butter and chopped basil. Yields 6 servings.

Veal Chops with Blackberries

Accompany this dish with oven-roasted potato slices, green beans with jicama and a Scharffenberger Blanc du Noir. You can use other berries in season or stir a little cream into the sauce just before serving if desired.

~ 6 (1-inch) veal loin chops, trimmed
~ Flour
~ Salt and pepper to taste
~ 1 1/2 tablespoons unsalted butter
~ 1 1/2 tablespoons safflower oil
~ 5 large shallots, chopped
~ 2 small carrots, peeled, coarsely shredded
~ 1/2 cup dry white wine
~ 1 cup chicken stock
~ 1 cup fresh or frozen blackberries

Sprinkle the veal chops with flour, salt and pepper, shaking off the excess. Brown on both sides in the heated butter and oil in a covered ovenproof skillet. Remove to a platter. Sauté the shallots and carrots in the drippings in the skillet until tender. Stir in the wine and cook until bubbly. Add the chicken stock and bring to a simmer. Add the veal chops and baste well. Bake, covered, at 325 degrees for 1 hour. Remove the chops to a heated platter. Cook the sauce until slightly reduced. Stir in the blackberries and correct the seasoning. Spoon over the chops. Yields 6 servings.

Veal Loin with Green Peppercorn Sauce

Greg Maser and Michael Bradley, Chefs at Hospital Trust Bank, have shared this delicious recipe.

~ 2 (6-ounce) veal loins
~ Tomato paste
~ Fresh thyme leaves
~ Salt
~ Freshly cracked green peppercorns to taste
~ Clarified butter
~ 1 cup red wine
~ 2 cups veal stock or light brown sauce
~ 1 tablespoon green peppercorns
~ Cream

Coat the veal with tomato paste and sprinkle with thyme, salt and cracked pepper. Place in a dish and chill for 1 hour or longer. Sear the veal on both sides in butter in a sauté pan. Remove to a baking dish. Bake at 375 degrees for 10 minutes. Add the wine to the sauté pan, stirring to deglaze. Stir in the veal stock. Cook until reduced by 1/2. Strain the mixture if using veal stock. Add the whole peppercorns and just enough cream to lighten the sauce. Yields 2 servings.

Veal Medallions in a Basil Crust with Roasted Garlic Cream Sauce

Serve this elegant dish with a Sakonnet Estate Chardonnay.

~ 2 pounds veal
  medallions
~ 2 cups bread crumbs
~ 3/4 cup chopped
  fresh basil leaves
~ 1 teaspoon salt

~ 1/2 teaspoon pepper
~ Milk
~ 1/2 cup olive oil
~ Roasted Garlic
  Cream Sauce
  (page 95)

~ 6 tablespoons pine
  nuts
~ 1/2 cup grated
  Parmesan cheese

Combine the bread crumbs, basil, salt and pepper in a dish. Dip the veal into the milk and then coat with the bread crumb mixture. Brown in the heated olive oil in a skillet over medium-high heat for one to two minutes on both sides; transfer to a warm platter. Spoon the Garlic Cream Sauce over the veal and sprinkle with the pine nuts and cheese. Serve immediately. Yields 6 servings.

Veal Scallopini Alessio

A Letrari Marzimino, 1993, from Trentino-Alto Adige goes well with this dish from Fabrizio Iannucci of Il Piccoli and Pizzico Restaurants.

~ 12 slices veal
~ Flour
~ 2 ounces unsalted
  butter
~ 1 tablespoon pine
  nuts, toasted
~ 1 sprig of rosemary
~ 8 large shiitake
  mushrooms

~ 1 red bell pepper,
  roasted, peeled, cut
  into strips
~ 1 yellow bell pepper,
  roasted, peeled, cut
  into strips
~ 1 tablespoon
  whole-grain
  mustard

~ 1 tablespoon red
  pepper jelly
~ 2 ounces cognac
~ Cream
~ Salt and white
  pepper to taste
~ 5 sprigs of Italian
  parsley, finely
  chopped

Pound the veal until very thin and coat with flour. Sauté on both sides in the butter in a sauté pan. Add the pine nuts, chopped rosemary, mushrooms and bell peppers. Sauté for 3 minutes. Stir in the mustard and pepper jelly. Add the cognac and ignite. Stir in the cream, salt and white pepper. Cook for one minute. Sprinkle with the parsley before serving. Yields 4 servings.

Involtini di Vitello Tuscany

Gaetano D'Urso at Capriccio Restaurant contributed this Italian dish. He recommends a Chianti Classico with it.

~ 2 (3-ounce) Italian sausages
~ 4 (4-ounce) veal scallopini
~ 4 large sage leaves
~ 1 red onion, chopped
~ 1 stalk celery, chopped
~ 1 medium carrot, chopped
~ 1 small clove of garlic, chopped
~ 1/2 cup olive oil
~ 1 cup dry white wine
~ Salt and pepper to taste
~ 1 pound fresh tomatoes, chopped

Remove the casing from the sausages and cut into halves. Pound the veal until thin. Top each with a sausage half and sage leaf. Roll to enclose the filling and secure with string. Sauté the onion, celery, carrot and garlic in the heated olive in a skillet over medium heat for 5 minutes. Add the veal rolls. Sauté for 5 minutes. Add the wine, salt and pepper. Cook for 5 minutes to reduce the sauce. Remove the veal to a warm dish and cover with foil. Add the tomatoes to the skillet and cook for 25 minutes. Process the mixture in a food mill and strain into the skillet. Add the veal rolls. Simmer, covered, for 15 minutes. Yields 4 servings.

Rabbit Stew with Capers

Chef Fabrizio Iannucci recommends a Sardinian Sella and Mosca Cannonau di Sardegna, 1989, to go with this dish from Il Piccolo and Pizzico Restaurants.

~ 1 rabbit, cut up
~ Salt and pepper to taste
~ 3 tablespoons olive oil
~ 1 shallot, chopped
~ 2 cloves of garlic, finely chopped
~ 2 tomatoes, chopped
~ 3 tablespoons capers
~ 1 sprig of rosemary
~ Oregano to taste
~ 10 leaves of Italian parsley, chopped
~ 1 cup dry white wine
~ 3 tablespoons white wine vinegar
~ 5 cups chicken stock

Sprinkle the rabbit with salt and pepper. Brown in the olive oil in a Dutch oven. Remove to a dish and drain the skillet. Add the shallot and garlic to the skillet and sauté until golden brown. Add the rabbit and next 7 ingredients. Cook for 5 minutes. Add the chicken stock. Bake, covered, at 375 degrees for 40 minutes. Yields 4 servings.

The village of Watch
Hill, one of the
state's outstanding
historic summer
resorts, takes its
name from a watch
tower built there to
sight enemies. By
the middle of the
19th century, it had
become an exclusive
summer resort, with
its beach considered
one of the finest in
New England. Grand
hotels and Victorian
summer cottages
housed the wealthy
summer residents,
who came from New
York and points west
by rail and steamer.
In addition to

Angel of Hearts

Add color to this dish with spinach or tomato pasta. Serve it with a
Stonington Vineyards Estate Chardonnay.

~ 4 (6-ounce)
 boneless skinless
 chicken breasts
~ 1 cup flour
~ 6 cloves of garlic,
 minced
~ 1 cup julienned
 portobello or
 shiitake mushrooms

~ 1/4 cup extra-virgin
 olive oil
~ 1 1/2 cups quartered
 artichoke hearts
~ 1/2 cup sweet
 vermouth
~ 1 cup
 reduced-sodium
 chicken broth

~ 1/4 cup lemon juice
~ 1 cup heavy cream
~ 1 cup grated
 Parmesan cheese
~ 12 to 16 ounces
 uncooked dried
 angel hair or
 capellini
~ Salt to taste

Cut the chicken into one-inch strips; rinse and pat dry. Coat with the
flour. Sauté the garlic and mushrooms in the olive oil in a skillet.
Remove to a warm dish with a slotted spoon. Add the chicken and sauté
until golden brown. Remove to the dish with the mushrooms. Add the
artichokes and sauté until golden brown. Remove to the dish with the
mushrooms and chicken. Add the wine to the skillet, stirring to deglaze.
Stir in the chicken broth and lemon juice. Cook until bubbly. Add the
cream, cheese and chicken and mushroom mixture; mix gently. Simmer
for 5 minutes, stirring frequently. Cook the pasta in salted boiling water
in a saucepan for 6 minutes or until al dente; drain. Place on a large
serving platter. Top with the chicken and sauce. Serve immediately.
Yields 4 to 6 servings.

water sports and the lovely walk to Napatree Point, the area boasted the Flying Horse Carousel. Probably the oldest working carousel in America, it continues to enthrall children of all ages.

Roasted Chicken with Mustard and Honey Glaze

This simple but elegant roasted chicken is good with or without the glaze suggested here. You may also baste and serve it with a gravy made by deglazing the pan with water and thickening the liquid.

~ 1 (7-pound) roasting chicken
~ 1 orange, cut into quarters
~ 1 small onion, cut into quarters
~ 2 teaspoons dried rosemary
~ Salt and pepper to taste
~ 1/2 cup water
~ Mustard and Honey Glaze (below)

Rinse the chicken inside and out and pat dry. Squeeze the juice from the orange quarters over the chicken and inside the cavity. Place the squeezed quarters and onion in the cavity and truss the chicken. Sprinkle with the rosemary, salt and pepper. Place breast side up in a roasting pan. Add the water. Roast at 400 degrees for 20 minutes. Reduce the oven temperature to 350 degrees and roast for one hour. Brush with the Mustard and Honey Glaze. Bake for 40 minutes or until golden brown. Yields 4 to 6 servings.

Mustard and Honey Glaze

~ 3 tablespoons melted butter
~ 3 tablespoons coarse- grain Dijon mustard
~ 3 tablespoons honey
~ 1 tablespoon apricot jam
~ 3 tablespoons orange liqueur or orange juice
~ Grated orange zest (optional)

Combine the butter, mustard, honey and apricot jam in a saucepan and mix well. Cook until heated through, stirring to mix well. Remove from the heat and stir in the liqueur and orange zest. Yields 4 to 6 servings.

The city of
Woonsocket, located
on the Blackstone
River, was initially
settled in 1698, but
developed into a
major industrial
center during the
19th century. The
Bernon Mill
complex was begun
in 1832 by
brothers-in-law
Sullivan Dorr and
Crawford Allen,
two very staunch
members of the
temperance
movement. These
men, in a most
unusual move, made
it possible for their
mill workers to

Sabra Chicken

The olives used in this recipe give it a Mediterranean flavor. Serve it with a Chateau Fombrauge (St. Emilion), 1990, or a Fransician Chardonnay, 1992.

~ 10 oil-cured olives
~ 3/4 cup water
~ 1 cup flour
~ 1/2 teaspoon paprika
~ 1 teaspoon salt
~ 1/2 teaspoon pepper

~ 2 chickens, cut into quarters
~ 2 cups orange juice
~ 1 cup dry red wine
~ 2 large red onions, sliced

~ 1 1/2 teaspoons thyme
~ 2 teaspoons salt
~ 1/4 teaspoon pepper
~ 1/2 cup slivered oil-cured olives

Simmer 10 olives in the water in a saucepan for 10 minutes. Strain and reserve the liquid. Mix the flour, paprika, salt and pepper together. Rinse the chicken and pat dry. Coat with the flour mixture and arrange in a single layer in a large shallow roasting pan. Combine the reserved olive liquid with the orange juice, wine, onion, thyme, salt and pepper in a saucepan and mix well. Simmer for 3 minutes. Pour over the chicken. Bake at 350 degrees for one hour, basting every 15 minutes. Spread the slivered olives over the top. Bake for 30 minutes longer. Yields 8 servings.

own a house lot in
the Bernon Mill
village, provided
the worker signed
an easement
prohibiting the
consumption of
alcoholic beverages
on his property. A
mineral spring
was discovered in
1858 at the nearby
Jillson family farm
and the family
started the Holly
Mineral Spring
Farm bottled water
business, which
continues today.

Cranberried Chicken Breast

This dish is excellent over rice. It could also be prepared with turkey and is a great way to use holiday leftovers. Serve it with Ecard Savigny Les Beaunes or a Liparita Chardonnay, 1992.

~ 6 boneless skinless
  chicken breast halves
~ 3/4 teaspoon salt
~ 1/4 teaspoon pepper

~ 3 tablespoons
  margarine
~ 2 1/4 cups cranberry
  juice

~ 3/4 cup whole
  cranberry sauce
~ 1/2 cup fresh or
  frozen cranberries

Rinse the chicken and pat dry. Sprinkle with the salt and pepper. Brown in the margarine in a skillet over high heat for 3 minutes on each side. Remove to a platter and keep warm. Add the cranberry juice and cranberry sauce in the skillet. Cook for 10 to 12 minutes. Add the cranberries. Simmer for 2 minutes or until the berries pop. Spoon over the chicken to serve. Yields 4 servings.

Lemon Chicken

Lemon Chicken is an easy dish to prepare in a slow cooker. It is great with rice pilaf and a Sakonnet America's Cup White wine.

~ 2 1/2 to 3 pounds
  cut-up chicken or
  chicken breasts
~ 1/4 cup flour
~ 1 1/4 teaspoons salt
~ 2 tablespoons
  vegetable oil

~ 1 (6-ounce) can
  frozen lemonade
  concentrate, thawed
~ 3 tablespoons
  brown sugar
~ 3 tablespoons catsup
~ 1 tablespoon vinegar

~ 2 tablespoons cold
  water
~ 2 tablespoons
  cornstarch

Rinse the chicken and pat dry. Coat with a mixture of the flour and salt. Brown on all sides in the heated oil in a skillet. Remove to a slow cooker. Combine the lemonade concentrate, brown sugar, catsup and vinegar in a bowl and mix well. Pour over the chicken. Cook on High for 3 to 4 hours or until cooked through. Drain the cooking liquid into a saucepan and skim the grease from the surface. Blend the water into the cornstarch in a cup. Add to the hot cooking liquid. Cook until thickened, stirring constantly. Serve with the chicken. Yields 6 servings.

Chicken Chili

Enjoy this with corn bread over steamed rice, with a Meridian Pinot Noir, 1990, or a Trimbach Riesling, 1992.

~ 6 boneless skinless chicken breasts
~ 1 cup coarsely chopped onion
~ 2 cloves of garlic, minced
~ 1/2 green bell pepper, chopped
~ 1/2 red bell pepper, chopped
~ 1/4 cup olive oil
~ 2 (16-ounce) cans Mexican-style stewed tomatoes
~ 1/2 cup medium picante sauce
~ 1 (16-ounce) can pinto beans or kidney beans
~ 1 teaspoon ground cumin
~ 1 teaspoon chili powder

Cut the chicken into bite-size pieces; rinse well and pat dry. Sauté the chicken, onion, garlic and bell peppers in the heated olive oil in a large sauté pan. Add the remaining ingredients and mix well. Simmer for 25 to 30 minutes or until done to taste. Yields 4 to 6 servings.

Chicken with Dijon and Sherry Sauce

Serve this with confetti rice and green beans with a vinaigrette dressing. Add a Mondavi Pinot Noir, 1992, or a Jean Fichet Bourgogne Aligotte, 1993.

~ 15 boneless skinless chicken breast halves
~ Salt and pepper to taste
~ 7 1/2 tablespoons butter
~ 30 ounces mushrooms, sliced
~ 3 3/4 medium onions, finely chopped
~ 3 3/4 tablespoons green peppercorns
~ 4 2/3 cups reduced-sodium chicken broth
~ 2 1/2 cups whipping cream
~ 7 1/2 tablespoons sherry
~ 5 1/2 tablespoons Dijon mustard

Rinse the chicken and pat dry; sprinkle with salt and pepper. Cook in the butter in a heavy skillet over medium heat for 4 minutes on each side. Remove to a platter. Add the mushrooms, onions and peppercorns to the skillet and sauté for 7 minutes or until the onion is tender. Stir in the chicken broth, cream, wine and mustard. Simmer until reduced to the desired consistency, stirring to deglaze the skillet. Add the chicken and accumulated juices. Cook until heated through. Yields 15 servings.

Garlic Chicken with Red Pepper

If you don't care for spicy Szechuan-style dishes, try this without the red pepper. A Chiario Barola, 1989, or a Tiefenbrunner Pinot Grigio, 1993, is recommended.

~ 1 tablespoon soy sauce
~ 1 tablespoon dry sherry
~ 1 to 1 1/2 tablespoons cornstarch
~ 2 tablespoons water
~ 1 pound boneless skinless chicken breasts

~ 2 tablespoons soy sauce
~ 2 tablespoons sugar
~ 2 teaspoons vinegar
~ 2 teaspoons sesame oil
~ 2 teaspoons cornstarch
~ 2 teaspoons water
~ 1/2 teaspoon salt

~ 10 small pieces red pepper
~ 8 cloves of garlic, minced
~ 1 can sliced water chestnuts, drained
~ 1 bunch green onions, chopped

Mix one tablespoon soy sauce, sherry, cornstarch and 2 tablespoons water in a shallow dish. Cut the chicken into one-inch cubes; rinse and pat dry. Add to the marinade and mix well. Marinate for 30 minutes. Combine 2 tablespoons soy sauce, sugar, vinegar, sesame oil, cornstarch, 2 teaspoons water and salt in a bowl and mix well; set aside. Stir-fry the undrained chicken in the oil in a skillet for several minutes. Add the red pepper and garlic. Add the cornstarch mixture and water chestnuts. Cook until thickened, stirring constantly. Remove the red pepper pieces. Add the green onions. Serve over rice. Yields 4 servings.

The Eleazar Arnold House, 1687, is a Rhode Island "stone-ender" and is regarded by architectural historians as the best preserved 17th century house in the state. The house is located on Great Road in Lincoln. Great Road, completed in 1683 and still in daily use today, is considered to be one of the most historic byways in the United States.

Honey-Baked Chicken

Family dinner is a special event with Honey-Baked Chicken served with Sesame Broccoli (page 139) and couscous. For company, add a Sakonnet Gewürztraminer.

~ 8 boneless skinless chicken breast halves
~ 1/4 cup butter
~ 1/2 cup honey
~ 1/4 cup Dijon mustard
~ 1 teaspoon curry powder
~ 1 teaspoon salt

Rinse the chicken and pat dry; arrange in a shallow baking pan. Melt the butter in a small saucepan. Whisk in the honey, mustard, curry powder and salt. Pour over the chicken. Bake at 350 degrees for 1 1/4 to 1 1/2 hours or until the chicken is tender and golden brown, basting every 15 minutes. Yields 6 to 8 servings.

Chicken Marsala

This dish can easily be increased to serve a crowd. Complement it with a chilled Chardonnay.

~ 1/4 cup flour
~ 1/4 teaspoon paprika
~ 1/4 teaspoon pepper
~ 2 boneless skinless chicken breasts
~ 1/4 cup margarine or butter or 2 tablespoons margarine and 2 tablespoons olive oil
~ 1/2 cup marsala
~ 1 cup sliced mushrooms
~ 2 tablespoons chopped parsley

Mix the flour, paprika and pepper together. Rinse the chicken and pat dry. Coat with the flour mixture. Sauté in the margarine in a heated skillet over low heat until golden brown and the juices run clear. Remove to an oven-proof platter and keep warm in a 200 degree oven. Add the wine to the skillet, stirring to deglaze. Add the mushrooms. Cook until the liquid is reduced by 1/2. Add any accumulated juices from the chicken. Spoon over the chicken. Top with the parsley. Yields 2 servings.

Mexican Chicken Torte

If time permits, make the refried beans by cooking dried black beans in chicken broth, heating in a skillet with sautéed onion, chile peppers and garlic and processing with some of the cooking liquid.

- ~ 4 boneless skinless chicken breasts
- ~ 3 tablespoons vegetable oil
- ~ 1 envelope taco seasoning mix or a mixture of chili powder, cumin, onion salt and garlic salt
- ~ 1 cup water
- ~ 2 cups shredded Cheddar cheese
- ~ 2 cups shredded Monterey Jack cheese
- ~ 6 (10-inch) flour tortillas
- ~ 2 cups refried black beans or canned refried beans
- ~ 1 bunch scallions, thinly sliced
- ~ 2 cups mild salsa
- ~ 1/4 head iceburg lettuce, shredded
- ~ 3 plum tomatoes, chopped
- ~ 1 avocado, chopped
- ~ 1/2 cup sour cream

Cut the chicken into one-inch cubes; rinse and pat dry. Brown in several batches in the heated oil in a skillet over medium-high heat. Combine the chicken in the skillet and reduce the heat to medium-low; drain. Stir in the taco seasoning mix and water. Simmer, covered, for 5 minutes. Reserve 1/3 of the cheeses. Arrange 2 tortillas in a 9x13-inch baking dish. Spread with 1/3 of the beans. Layer the chicken, scallions, cheeses, a small amount of salsa and remaining tortillas 1/2 at a time in the prepared dish. Top with the reserved cheeses. Bake at 350 degrees for 10 minutes or until the cheese melts and begins to brown. Spoon the remaining salsa over the top. Sprinkle with the lettuce, tomatoes and avocado. Spoon the sour cream over the top. *Yields 8 servings.*

Double-Crust Chicken and Cheese Pie

This is great for picnics, as it can be served hot or cold. It even went on the Newport to Bermuda Race.

~ Double-Crust Pastry (below)
~ 2 cups chopped cooked chicken
~ 2 eggs, beaten
~ 2 cups shredded Swiss cheese
~ 1/4 cup chopped fresh parsley
~ 2 tablespoons chopped green chiles
~ 1/4 teaspoon paprika
~ 1/8 teaspoon onion powder
~ 1 egg, lightly beaten
~ 1 tablespoon water
~ 1 teaspoon poppy seeds

Roll each portion of dough to a 13-inch circle on a floured surface. Place one portion on a greased 12-inch pizza pan. Combine the chicken, 2 eggs, cheese, parsley, green chiles, paprika and onion powder in a bowl and mix well. Spread in the prepared pan. Top with the remaining pastry; flute the edge and prick the top with a fork. Cover tightly with foil and bake at 400 degrees for 55 minutes. Brush with a mixture of one egg and water; sprinkle with the poppy seeds. Bake, uncovered, for 15 to 20 minutes longer or until golden brown. Cut into wedges to serve. Wrap in foil to store in the refrigerator or freezer. Yields 6 to 8 servings.

Double-Crust Pastry

~ 1 envelope dry yeast
~ 2/3 cup (110 to 115 degree) water
~ 2 to 2 1/4 cups flour
~ 1/2 teaspoon sugar
~ 1/2 teaspoon salt
~ 2 tablespoons vegetable oil

Dissolve the yeast in the warm water in a bowl. Mix one cup flour, sugar and salt in a bowl. Add the yeast and oil and mix well. Stir in enough of the remaining flour to form a medium-stiff dough. Knead on a lightly floured surface for 5 to 8 minutes or until smooth and elastic. Place in a greased bowl, turning to coat the surface. Let rise, covered, in a warm place for one hour or until doubled in bulk. Punch dough down and divide into 2 portions. Let rest, covered, for 10 minutes. Yields 2 pastries.

Chicken Potpie

Serve with an Ecard Savigny Les Beaudes or a Liparita Chardonnay, 1992.

- ~ 2 1/2 pounds cut-up chicken, skinned
- ~ 9 cups water
- ~ 3 stalks celery, cut into 4 pieces each
- ~ 1 small onion, cut into quarters
- ~ 1 bay leaf
- ~ 1 tablespoon peppercorns
- ~ 1/2 cup chopped celery
- ~ 1 1/2 cups chopped unpeeled red potatoes
- ~ 1/2 cup chopped red bell pepper
- ~ 1 clove of garlic, minced
- ~ 3/4 cup sliced carrot
- ~ 1/2 cup chopped leek
- ~ 1 cup sliced mushrooms
- ~ 1/2 cup frozen green peas
- ~ 6 tablespoons flour
- ~ 1 teaspoon poultry seasoning
- ~ 1/2 teaspoon salt
- ~ 1/4 teaspoon pepper
- ~ 1 cup low-fat milk
- ~ Biscuit Topping (below)

Rinse the chicken. Combine with the next 5 ingredients in an 8-quart stockpot. Simmer for one hour. Remove the chicken to a bowl and chill for 15 minutes. Strain the broth and reserve 4 1/2 cups; chop the chicken. Bring the reserved broth to a boil in a large saucepan over medium-high heat. Add the chopped celery, potatoes, bell pepper and garlic. Cook, covered, for 5 minutes. Add the carrot and leek. Cook, covered, for 3 minutes. Add the mushrooms and peas. Cook, covered, for 5 minutes or until the vegetables are tender. Whisk the flour, poultry seasoning, salt, pepper and milk in a bowl. Add to the saucepan. Cook over medium heat for 3 minutes or until thickened, stirring constantly. Add the chicken. Spoon into a 9x13-inch baking dish sprayed with nonstick cooking spray. Drop the Biscuit Topping into 16 mounds on top. Bake at 400 degrees for 28 minutes or until golden brown. *Yields 8 servings.*

Biscuit Topping

- ~ 2 cups flour
- ~ 2 teaspoons baking powder
- ~ 1/4 teaspoon sugar
- ~ 1/8 teaspoon garlic powder
- ~ 1 cup low-fat milk
- ~ 1 1/2 tablespoons melted margarine

Mix the flour, baking powder, sugar, garlic powder and salt to taste in a bowl. Add the milk and margarine and mix well. *Yields 8 servings.*

The John Brown
House, 1785,
designed by Joseph
Brown in the
Georgian style, was
described by Abigail
Adams as "one of
the grandest I have
seen in the country.
Everything in and
about it wore
the marks of
magnificence and
taste." Her son,
John Quincy Adams,
characterized the
house as "the most
magnificent and
elegant private
mansion I have
ever seen on this
continent." The
interior restoration
by the Rhode Island

Southwestern Chicken Potpie

You will like the zip that the crust gives to this updated version of a traditional favorite.

~ 1 (3-pound) chicken
~ 3 cups water
~ 1 tablespoon instant chicken bouillon
~ 1/2 teaspoon pepper
~ 1 cup chopped potatoes

~ 1 cup chopped carrots
~ 1 cup chopped celery
~ 18 small whole pearl onions
~ 1/4 cup whole wheat flour

~ 1/4 cup melted butter
~ 1 1/2 tablespoons minced fresh cilantro
~ Southwestern Topping (below)

Cut up the chicken and rinse well. Combine with the water, instant bouillon and pepper in a 5-quart saucepan. Simmer for 40 minutes. Drain, reserving the broth; chop the chicken. Strain the broth into the saucepan and add the vegetables. Simmer for 10 minutes or until the vegetables are just tender. Drain, reserving 2 cups broth. Blend the flour into the butter in a saucepan. Cook over low heat for one to two minutes, stirring constantly. Whisk in the reserved broth gradually. Cook over low heat for 10 minutes or until thickened, stirring frequently. Add 1 1/2 tablespoons cilantro, chicken and vegetables. Spoon into a buttered 9-inch baking dish. Arrange the topping wedges over the top. Bake at 425 degrees for 20 minutes or until golden brown. Yields 6 servings.

Southwestern Topping

~ 1/2 cup stone-ground cornmeal
~ 1/2 cup whole wheat flour

~ 1/2 cup unbleached flour
~ 1 tablespoon baking powder
~ 3 tablespoons butter

~ 1 tablespoon minced jalapeño pepper
~ 1/2 cup shredded Cheddar cheese
~ 1/2 cup buttermilk

Mix the dry ingredients in a bowl. Cut in the butter until crumbly. Add the pepper and cheese. Warm the buttermilk in a saucepan. Add to the flour mixture and mix well. Knead 5 times on a lightly floured surface. Pat into a circle 1 1/2 inches thick and 2 inches smaller than the baking dish. Cut into 6 wedges. Yields 6 servings.

Chicken Saltimbocca

These can be served whole or sliced, with a Sakonnet Rhode Island Red.

~ 8 boneless skinless chicken breast halves
~ 2 teaspoons minced garlic
~ 1/2 cup grated Parmesan cheese
~ 2 teaspoons kosher salt
~ 2 teaspoons pepper
~ 8 slices prosciutto
~ 1/2 cup marsala
~ 1/4 cup olive oil
~ 2 cups sliced mushrooms
~ 1 cup marinara sauce
~ 1 cup chicken stock

Rinse the chicken and pat dry; sprinkle with half the garlic, cheese, salt and pepper. Pound to 1 1/2 times their original size between waxed paper. Layer the prosciutto over the chicken and sprinkle with the remaining cheese. Drizzle with half the wine. Roll the chicken to enclose the filling. Arrange seam side down in a 9x13-inch baking dish. Sauté the remaining garlic with the remaining salt and pepper in the heated olive oil in a large skillet. Add the mushrooms. Sauté until tender and lightly browned. Add the marinara sauce, remaining wine and chicken stock. Simmer for 5 minutes. Pour over the chicken rolls. Bake, covered, at 350 degrees for 45 minutes. Yields 4 to 8 servings.

Chicken Twists

~ 3 ounces cream cheese
~ 2 tablespoons butter, softened
~ 2 tablespoons milk
~ 2 cups chopped cooked chicken
~ 1 tablespoon minced onion
~ 1 (2-ounce) can mushrooms
~ 1/4 teaspoon salt
~ 1/2 teaspoon pepper
~ 1 can crescent rolls
~ 1 tablespoon melted butter
~ 1/3 cup crushed herb-seasoned croutons

Blend the cream cheese, 2 tablespoons butter and milk in a bowl. Add the chicken, onion, mushrooms, salt and pepper and mix well. Separate the roll dough into 4 rectangles, pressing perforations to seal. Roll each into a 5x6-inch rectangle on a floured surface. Spoon the chicken mixture into the centers. Pull the corners up to enclose the filling and twist to seal. Place on a baking sheet. Brush with the butter and sprinkle with the crushed croutons. Bake at 350 degrees for 20 to 25 minutes or until golden brown. Yields 4 servings.

The Nightingale-
Brown House,
built in 1791 in
the Federal style,
is the largest
wooden residence
remaining from the
18th century in
the country.

Cornish Game Hens with Dijon Peach Glaze

This elegant dish comes from the Gourmet Dining Workshops of Richard and Claudette Brodeur's Aaron Smith Farm.

~ 1 cup cooked sausage, drained
~ 4 cups seasoned bread cubes
~ Sage, salt and pepper to taste
~ 1/4 cup butter
~ 4 Cornish game hens
~ Dijon Peach Glaze (below)

Combine the sausage with the bread cubes, sage, salt and pepper in a bowl. Melt the butter in a saucepan. Add to the stuffing with enough water to moisten and toss lightly. Rinse the game hens inside and out, discarding the gizzards and livers; pat dry. Stuff loosely with the stuffing mixture and secure the cavities with wooden picks. Brush with the Dijon Peach Glaze and place in a baking pan. Roast at 350 degrees for 1 1/2 hours or until cooked through, basting occasionally. Yields 4 servings.

Dijon Peach Glaze

~ 1 cup peach preserves or jam
~ 1/4 cup barbecue sauce
~ 1/2 teaspoon Dijon mustard
~ 1/2 teaspoon nutmeg
~ 1/2 teaspoon cinnamon

Combine the preserves, barbecue sauce, mustard, nutmeg and cinnamon in a 2-quart saucepan and heat over medium heat, stirring to mix well.

A Tasteful

Reflection of

Historic

Rhode Island

Seafood

Seafood

Shellfish

New England-Style Flounder en Papillote

This is a specialty of the La France Restaurant. Serve it with a good French rosé such as Moc Baril Rosé D'Anjou or a full-bodied California chardonnay such as Acacia Canares Chardonnay.

~ 4 (6- to 8-ounce) flounder fillets
~ 2 cups water
~ Juice of 1 lemon
~ 2 bay leaves
~ Thyme to taste
~ 1 teaspoon salt
~ 1/2 teaspoon pepper

~ 2 tablespoons butter
~ 2 tablespoons flour
~ 1/2 cup thinly sliced mushrooms
~ 12 cooked medium shrimp
~ 12 cherrystone clams or mussels

~ 4 green onions, chopped
~ 2 cloves of garlic, chopped
~ 1/2 cup dry white wine

Combine the flounder with the water, lemon juice, bay leaves, thyme, salt and pepper in a saucepan. Poach for 5 minutes. Remove the fillets with a slotted spatula and place each on a rectangle of buttered baking parchment paper. Strain the poaching liquid. Melt the butter in a saucepan and stir in the flour. Stir in the poaching liquid gradually and cook until the mixture thickens, stirring constantly. Add the mushrooms, shrimp, clams, green onions and garlic. Cook until bubbly. Stir in the wine. Spoon the sauce and seafood over the fish and fold the parchment to enclose it completely, sealing the edges tightly. Place on a baking sheet. Bake at 400 degrees for 15 minutes or until the fish is cooked through. Yields 4 servings.

Dentice alla Giuda

Thanks for this recipe from the Italian Jewish tradition go to Walter Potenza of the Sunflower Cafe. Serve it with chick-peas or buttered lupini beans.

- ~ 1 (6-pound) or 2 (3-pound) red snapper
- ~ 1/4 cup balsamic vinegar
- ~ 1/2 cup olive oil
- ~ 1 cup dry white wine
- ~ 2 teaspoons sugar
- ~ 2 cloves of garlic, minced
- ~ 2 ounces capers, rinsed
- ~ 1 teaspoon salt
- ~ 10 escarole leaves, cut into strips

Clean and fillet the fish, reserving the head and bones. Combine the fish trimmings with the vinegar, olive oil, wine, sugar, garlic, capers and salt in a saucepan. Simmer, covered, for 30 minutes. Strain the stock through a fine sieve. Place the fish in a baking dish and sprinkle with the escarole. Pour the strained stock over the top. Bake at 400 degrees for 30 minutes. Yields 6 to 8 servings.

Salmon in Red Wine Sauce

A Sakonnet Pinot Noir goes well with this dish. If the sauce should break down at any time, remove it from the heat and whisk in two tablespoons of cold butter and strain it.

- ~ 1 1/4 cups dry red wine
- ~ 5 tablespoons red wine vinegar
- ~ 2 shallots, minced
- ~ 4 sprigs of thyme
- ~ 1 tablespoon unsalted butter
- ~ 1 tablespoon olive oil
- ~ 6 (8-ounce) salmon fillets, 3/4 inch thick, skinned
- ~ 12 tablespoons unsalted butter, chilled, sliced into 1 tablespoon portions

Bring the wine, vinegar, shallots and thyme to a boil in a small heavy saucepan and cook for 15 minutes or until reduced to 1/3 cup; discard the thyme. Set aside for up to 6 hours. Heat 1 tablespoon butter and the olive oil in a large heavy skillet over medium-high heat. Add 3 salmon fillets at a time and cook for 4 minutes on each side or until brown and cooked through; remove to a warm serving plate. Bring the wine sauce to a simmer and remove from the heat. Whisk in 2 tablespoons butter. Place over low heat and continue to whisk in the remaining 10 tablespoons butter one tablespoon at a time. Serve with the salmon. Yields 6 servings.

Souffléed Potato Crepes with Smoked Salmon and Savoy Cabbage

This recipe is from Chef/Owner Paul O'Connell of the Providence Restaurant in Brookline, Massachusetts.

~ 3 shallots, sliced
~ 1/2 cup melted butter
~ 4 cups thinly sliced savoy cabbage
~ 1/4 cup white wine

~ 1/2 cup sour cream
~ 1 bunch chives, chopped
~ Juice of 2 lemons

~ 12 ounces smoked salmon
~ Souffléed Potato Crepes (below)

Sauté the shallots in the melted butter in a sauté pan until translucent. Add the cabbage, tossing to coat well with the butter mixture and adding additional butter if needed. Sauté over medium heat until tender-crisp. Add the wine and cook until heated through. Remove from the heat and stir in the sour cream, chives, lemon juice and salmon. Spoon onto serving plates. Serve with the Souffléed Potato Crepes.
Yields 6 to 8 servings.

Souffléed Potato Crepes

~ 4 Idaho potatoes, baked
~ 1 1/2 cups milk, scalded
~ 2 eggs, beaten

~ 1 cup flour
~ 3 tablespoons melted butter
~ Salt and pepper to taste

~ 2 egg whites, stiffly beaten
~ 1/4 cup chopped scallions

Cut the potatoes into halves and scoop out the pulp. Rice the pulp with a food mill or canister ricer. Whisk a small amount of the hot milk into the eggs; whisk the eggs into the hot milk. Combine with the flour, butter, salt and pepper in a bowl and mix well. Fold in the riced potatoes and then the beaten egg whites. Heat a nonstick oven-proof skillet over medium heat and add a small amount of oil. Ladle about 2 ounces of the potato mixture at a time into the pan and sprinkle with the scallions. Fold the crepe over. Bake at 350 degrees for 4 minutes.
Yields 6 to 8 servings.

The Providence Arcade was America's first indoor shopping mall. This 1828 National Historic Landmark in the Greek Revival style, boasts six huge Ionic columns which were carved in single pieces from a granite quarry in Johnston, Rhode Island, and hauled to Providence by fifteen yoke of oxen; they still rank among the largest in the country.

Grilled Salmon Sandwich with Mustard Sauce

This is an easy way to impress guests for lunches, brunches or picnics.

~ 4 (6-ounce) salmon fillets
~ 2 teaspoons olive oil

~ Salt and freshly ground pepper to taste
~ 1/2 bunch arugula, washed

~ 4 slices sourdough bread, crusts trimmed, toasted
~ Mustard Sauce (below)

Brush the salmon with the olive oil and season with salt and pepper. Grill over very hot coals for 5 minutes on each side or until the fish flakes easily. Heat a small skillet over medium heat. Add the undrained arugula and season with salt and pepper. Cook, covered, for 2 minutes or until wilted, tossing occasionally. Place the toasted bread on individual serving plates. Top with the salmon and arugula. Drizzle with the mustard sauce. Yields 4 servings.

Mustard Sauce

~ 2 tablespoons dry mustard
~ 3 tablespoons brown sugar

~ 1 1/2 tablespoons water
~ 1 teaspoon olive oil

~ 1/2 teaspoon soy sauce

Mix the mustard and sugar in a small bowl. Add the water, olive oil and soy sauce and mix well.

Salmon in Parchment

This is a health-conscious colorful dish with a memorable presentation.
Serve it with Black Opal Chardonnay, 1994, or Auffray Chardonnay, 1992.

~ 1/2 cup chopped scallions

~ 4 teaspoons light margarine

~ 1 cup thinly sliced mushrooms

~ 1/2 teaspoon savory

~ 1 cup thinly sliced red bell pepper

~ 1/4 teaspoon marjoram

~ 1 1/2 cups snow peas

~ 1 1/2 cups cooked barley

~ 1/2 cup cooked wild rice

~ 4 (3-ounce) salmon fillets

~ 1/4 teaspoon salt

Sauté the scallions in the margarine in a medium nonstick skillet for 2
minutes. Add the mushrooms, savory, bell pepper and marjoram. Sauté
just until the vegetables are tender. Cut four 12-inch squares of parchment
into heart shapes. Combine the snow peas, barley and rice in a bowl and
mix well. Spoon onto one side of each piece of parchment and place the
fish on top; top with the vegetables and sprinkle with the salt. Fold the
parchment over to enclose the mixture and turn the edges over in an
overlapping seal. Place on a baking sheet. Bake at 400 degrees for 12
minutes or until the packets are puffed. Place the packets on serving
plates, slit open carefully and turn back the parchment to serve.
Yields 4 servings.

Fish Bundles

Serve fish bundles with Sakonnet Estate Chardonnay, 1992.

~ 4 (4-ounce) fresh or frozen sole or flounder fillets

~ 1/2 teaspoon lemon pepper

~ 1 small yellow squash

~ 1 small zucchini

~ 4 green onions

~ Paprika

Thaw frozen fish fillets and sprinkle with the lemon pepper. Cut the
yellow squash and zucchini into thin 2-inch sticks. Cut the green onions
into 2 1/2-inch slivers. Arrange the vegetables into 4 bundles and place
crosswise on the fish fillets. Roll the fish to enclose the vegetables. Place
seam side down in a 2-quart baking dish and sprinkle with paprika. Bake,
covered, at 350 degrees for 25 minutes. Bake, uncovered, for 5 to 10
minutes longer or just until the fish flakes easily. Yields 4 servings.

Grilled Swordfish with Capers

Grill salad greens (page 56) at the same time to serve with this dish. Enjoy with a Chapoutier Belleruche Cotes du Rhône Blanc or a Ferrari Carano Chardonnay, 1993.

- ~ 4 (8-ounce) swordfish steaks, 1 inch thick
- ~ 1/2 cup olive oil
- ~ 2 tablespoons drained capers
- ~ 2 tablespoons lemon juice
- ~ 1 tablespoon chopped parsley
- ~ 2 oil-pack anchovy fillets
- ~ 2 cloves of garlic
- ~ 1/2 teaspoon pepper

Place the fish in an ungreased 7x12-inch dish. Combine the olive oil, capers, lemon juice, parsley, anchovies, garlic and pepper in a food processor or blender and process until smooth. Pour over the fish. Marinate, covered, in the refrigerator for one hour, turning after 30 minutes. Drain, reserving the marinade. Grill the fish 4 inches from hot coals for 10 to 15 minutes or until it flakes easily, turning once and brushing with the reserved marinade occasionally. Yields 4 servings.

Grilled Marinated Swordfish

Swordfish tends to be a dry fish and the marinade keeps it moist in this recipe that is easy to prepare, but special enough for company. Serve with a Westport Rivers Estate Chardonnay.

- ~ 4 (8-ounce) fresh swordfish steaks
- ~ 1 clove of garlic, minced
- ~ 1 tablespoon minced fresh ginger
- ~ Juice of 1 lime
- ~ 1/2 cup olive oil
- ~ 1/4 cup soy sauce
- ~ 1 tablespoon toasted sesame seeds
- ~ 1/2 teaspoon red pepper flakes

Place the fish in a shallow dish. Combine the garlic, ginger, lime juice, olive oil, soy sauce, sesame seeds and red pepper flakes in a bowl and mix well. Pour over the fish. Marinate, covered, at room temperature for 30 minutes or in the refrigerator for 4 hours; drain. Grill the fish over hot coals for 6 to 8 minutes or until a sharp knife inserted in the center feels no resistance. Yields 4 servings.

Stuffed Grilled Tuna Steaks with Salsa La France

David Gaudet at La France Restaurant has shared this delicious dish with us. Serve it with a Ferrari Carano Fumé, 1993, or a good Mexican beer.

~ 4 (1-inch thick) tuna steaks
~ Salt and pepper to taste

~ 1 cup shredded mozzarella cheese
~ 1 teaspoon sage

~ 2 cups Salsa La France (below)

Cut deep pockets in the side of each steak with a sharp knife. Sprinkle with the salt and pepper. Toss the cheese with the sage in a bowl. Stuff into the pockets in the fish. Broil or grill over hot coals for 5 to 7 minutes on each side or until the fish flakes easily. Serve with Salsa La France. Yields 4 servings.

Salsa La France

This makes more than you may need for the tuna steaks, but you will find many uses for this delicious salsa.

~ 10 tomatoes
~ 1 green bell pepper, chopped
~ 1 red bell pepper, chopped
~ 1 yellow bell pepper, chopped
~ 1 jalapeño pepper, chopped

~ 1 small red onion, chopped
~ 1 1/2 tablespoons chopped cilantro
~ 2 tablespoons chopped shallots
~ Chopped garlic to taste

~ 2 1/2 tablespoons olive oil
~ 1 tablespoon balsamic vinegar
~ Juice of 1/2 lime
~ Salt and pepper to taste

Core the tomatoes and cut an X on the bottoms. Immerse in boiling water for 30 seconds and remove the skin. Place in ice water until chilled. Chop the tomatoes. Combine with the bell peppers, jalapeño peppers, onion, cilantro, shallots, garlic, olive oil, vinegar, lime juice, salt and pepper in a bowl and mix well. Let stand for one hour or longer. Yields 12 cups.

Teriyaki Tuna with Fresh Pineapple

This is also delicious with swordfish or the Papaya and Red Pepper Relish (page 147). Serve with a Guigal Cotes Du Rhône Blanc, 1993, or Havens Sauvignon Blanc, 1993.

- ~ 1/4 cup reduced-sodium soy sauce
- ~ 3 tablespoons honey
- ~ 3 tablespoons mirin (sweet rice wine)
- ~ 2 teaspoons minced peeled gingerroot
- ~ 1/2 teaspoon hot sauce
- ~ 1 clove of garlic, minced
- ~ 1 small pineapple
- ~ 6 (4-ounce) tuna steaks, 3/4 inch thick
- ~ Green onions

Combine the soy sauce, honey, mirin, gingerroot, hot sauce and garlic in a large dish. Peel and core the pineapple and cut into 6 spears. Place the pineapple and the tuna in the dish and coat well. Marinate, covered, in the refrigerator for 30 minutes, turning every 10 minutes. Drain, reserving the marinade. Place the fish and pineapple on a grill rack sprayed with nonstick cooking spray. Grill over medium-hot coals for 4 minutes on each side for medium-rare or until done to taste, basting occasionally with reserved marinade. Garnish servings with green onions. Yields 6 servings.

Grilled Squid

This recipe comes from Raphael Bar·Risto on the River in Providence.

- ~ 1/2 cup olive oil
- ~ 1/2 cup white wine
- ~ 1 teaspoon salt
- ~ 1/2 teaspoon crushed red pepper
- ~ 1 teaspoon black pepper
- ~ 1 pound cleaned squid tubes, sliced lengthwise
- ~ 1 small onion, sliced
- ~ 1/2 bulb fennel, sliced
- ~ 4 hot cherry peppers, sliced
- ~ 1 lemon, cut into quarters

Combine the olive oil, wine, salt, red pepper and black pepper in a bowl and mix well. Add the squid and mix well. Marinate in the refrigerator for 4 hours or longer. Drain, reserving the marinade. Grill the squid over an open flame until it begins to brown, tossing frequently. Add the onion and fennel. Grill until cooked through, basting with the reserved marinade. Serve with hot peppers and lemon wedges. Yields 4 servings.

Edgar Allen Poe. Sarah Helen Whitman, who inspired Poe's poem "Annabelle Lee" was said to have rendezvoused with Poe in the stacks of the Antenaeum during their tempestuous courtship.

Clam Pie

This old family recipe has its origins in Newport. For added flavor, substitute clam juice for part of the milk in the white sauce. Serve it with a Westport Rivers Pinot Blanc.

~ 4 ounces mushrooms, sliced
~ 1 large onion, chopped
~ 1 stalk celery, chopped
~ 2 medium potatoes, chopped

~ 4 carrots, sliced
~ 1 green bell pepper, chopped
~ 12 large or 14 medium clams, shucked, chopped
~ 2 hard-cooked eggs, chopped

~ 1 1/2 cups white sauce
~ Salt and pepper to taste
~ 1 recipe (1-crust) pie pastry (page 68)

Combine the mushrooms, onion, celery, potatoes, carrots and green pepper with a small amount of water in a saucepan. Cook just until tender; drain. Combine with the clams, eggs, white sauce, salt and pepper in a bowl and mix well. Spoon into a buttered baking dish. Top with the pastry. Bake at 350 degrees for 30 to 45 minutes or until the top is golden brown. Yields 4 to 6 servings.

Linguini with Clams

Serve with bread for soaking up the sauce and a Sakonnet Chardonnay, 1993 Newport Series, or a Westport Pinot Blanc.

~ 3 to 4 dozen clams in the shell, scrubbed
~ 1/4 cup water
~ 3 cloves of garlic, minced
~ 1/2 small onion, finely chopped

~ 2 tablespoons butter
~ 2 tablespoons olive oil
~ 1/2 cup dry white wine
~ Salt and pepper to taste

~ 1/2 cup chopped fresh parsley
~ 8 ounces linguini, cooked

Steam the clams in the water until they open. Cool to room temperature and remove from the shells. Strain and reserve the broth. Sauté the garlic and onion in the melted butter and oil in a skillet. Add the wine and reserved broth and bring to a boil. Add the clams, salt, pepper and parsley. Spoon the pasta onto a serving platter. Top with the hot clam sauce. Yields 4 servings.

Lobster-Stuffed Potatoes

This makes a great first course, or serve it with a salad and crusty bread for a filling meal.

- ~ 6 medium to large red potatoes
- ~ Salt and pepper to taste
- ~ 3/4 cup chopped yellow onion
- ~ 1/4 cup unsalted butter
- ~ 3/4 cup finely chopped fresh mushrooms
- ~ 2 cups chopped cooked lobster or crab meat
- ~ 1 1/4 cups dry vermouth
- ~ 3/4 cup sour cream
- ~ 1 cup shredded Jarlsberg cheese
- ~ 1 to 2 tablespoons heavy cream

Cut a slit in the top of each potato and place on the center oven rack. Bake at 375 degrees for one hour or until tender. Cool the potatoes slightly. Cut a slice from the long side of each potato and discard. Scoop the pulp into a bowl, reserving the shells. Sprinkle the shells with salt and pepper. Mash the potato pulp. Cook the onion, covered, in the butter in a small skillet for 25 minutes or until caramelized. Add the mushrooms and sauté for 5 minutes. Stir in the lobster, vermouth, salt and pepper. Increase the heat. Cook until the liquid has evaporated, stirring frequently. Stir in the sour cream. Add the mashed potato pulp and 3/4 cup of the cheese and mix well. Adjust the seasonings and add one to 2 tablespoons heavy cream if needed for desired consistency. Spoon into the reserved shells, mounding the mixture slightly. Sprinkle with the remaining cheese. Bake at 400 degrees until the potatoes are heated through and the cheese is bubbly. Serve immediately. Yields 6 servings.

Angel Hair Pasta with Lobster Sauce

Fabrizio Iannucci of Il Piccolo and Pizzico Restaurants has contributed this recipe. Serve it with a McGuigans Semillon/Chardonnay, 1993.

~ 2 thin slices sweet red onion, chopped
~ 2 tablespoons unsalted butter
~ 1 tomato, chopped
~ 1 (1-pound) lobster, steamed, chopped

~ 1/2 cup heavy cream
~ 6 fresh basil leaves, chopped
~ Salt and white pepper to taste
~ 1/4 cup brandy

~ 8 ounces uncooked angel hair pasta or capellini, cooked
~ 2 tablespoons grated Parmesan cheese

Sauté the onion in the butter in a saucepan. Add the tomato and lobster. Sauté for 30 seconds. Add the cream, basil, salt, pepper and brandy. Cook for one minute. Add the pasta and cheese and mix gently. Spoon onto serving plates. Garnish with the lobster claws. Yields 2 servings.

Scallops Arlesciène

This dish from the La France Restaurant makes a beautiful presentation served in the scallop shells, but it is also delicious in puff pastry shells.

~ 5 shallots, minced
~ 8 ounces mushrooms, sliced
~ 1/4 cup capers, rinsed
~ 1 tablespoon butter
~ 3 tablespoons (or more) margarine

~ 1 1/2 pounds bay scallops
~ 1/2 cup flour
~ Salt and pepper to taste
~ 6 artichoke hearts, cut into quarters

~ 2 tablespoons sweet vermouth
~ 2 tablespoons dry vermouth
~ Juice and rind of 1/2 lemon
~ 1/4 cup heavy cream

Sauté the shallots, mushrooms and capers in the butter and margarine in a sauté pan for 3 minutes or until the mushrooms are tender. Remove with a slotted spoon. Coat the scallops with a mixture of the flour, salt and pepper. Add to the sauté pan and sauté until light brown, adding additional margarine if needed. Add the mushroom mixture and artichoke hearts, stirring to deglaze the pan. Stir in the vermouth, lemon juice and whole lemon rind. Simmer, covered, for one minute. Stir in the cream. Simmer for one minute longer. Discard the lemon rind. Yields 4 servings.

Greenwich Cove, a secure harbor in East Greenwich, was a shipping port until the War of 1812 and an excellent area for oysters, clams and scallops. This abundance created a permanent community of shellfishermen, who lived and worked along the cove in a group of shanties called "Scalloptown." Recent historic restoration has turned the area into a marina with many excellent waterfront restaurants.

(Conley 135)

Herbed Scallops with Vegetables

This attractive dish is ideal for entertaining. Serve it with a Palmer Vineyards Estate Chardonnay.

~ 1/2 cup julienned leeks
~ 1/2 cup julienned carrots
~ 1/2 cup julienned celery
~ 1/2 cup julienned fennel
~ 2 tablespoons butter or margarine
~ 1/2 cup white wine
~ 2 pounds bay scallops

~ 1/4 cup butter or margarine
~ 1 teaspoon chopped spinach
~ 1 teaspoon chopped parsley
~ 1 teaspoon chopped fresh tarragon or basil or 1/2 teaspoon dried tarragon or basil
~ 1 large clove of garlic, crushed

~ 1/4 teaspoon salt
~ 1/8 teaspoon pepper
~ 1 teaspoon flour
~ 1 tablespoon butter or margarine, softened
~ 6 frozen puff pastry shells, baked
~ Sprigs of parsley

Stir-fry the leeks, carrots, celery and fennel in 2 tablespoons butter in a skillet for one minute. Add the wine and simmer for 3 minutes; keep warm. Pat the scallops dry. Sauté the scallops in 1/4 cup butter in a large skillet over medium heat for 3 to 5 minutes or until cooked through. Add the spinach, one teaspoon parsley, tarragon, garlic, salt, pepper and the stir-fried vegetables; mix well. Blend the flour into the softened butter in a cup. Push the scallops and vegetables to one side of the skillet. Add one tablespoon butter and flour mixture and stir into the vegetables. Cook until slightly thickened, stirring gently. Spoon into the pastry shells and garnish with additional parsley. Yields 6 servings.

Baked Honey Scallops

Enjoy the sweet and tangy taste of this dish with a Newton Chardonnay, 1993, or an Auxey Duresses White, 1993.

- ~ 1 tablespoon mayonnaise
- ~ 1 tablespoon honey
- ~ 1/4 teaspoon garlic powder
- ~ 1/2 teaspoon salt
- ~ Pepper to taste
- ~ 2 cups sea scallops, cut into bite-size pieces
- ~ 3/4 cup crushed stuffing mix
- ~ Butter
- ~ Paprika to taste

Combine the mayonnaise and honey in a microwave-safe bowl and mix well. Microwave on High for 20 seconds. Stir in the garlic powder, salt and pepper. Add the scallops and mix to coat well. Spoon into a greased baking dish. Sprinkle with the stuffing mix, dot with butter and sprinkle with paprika. Bake at 350 degrees for 25 minutes or until bubbly and brown. Yields 2 servings.

Pappardelle with Scallops

Scallops are a special fall treat in New England because October and November are the best months for harvesting them. Chiarla Barbera d'Asti, 1993, or Tiefenbrunner Chardonnay, 1993, goes well with this scallops and pasta dish.

- ~ 1/4 cup chopped sun-dried tomatoes
- ~ Juice of 1/2 lemon
- ~ 1/4 cup olive oil
- ~ 1/4 cup grated Parmesan cheese
- ~ Salt and pepper to taste
- ~ 1 clove of garlic, crushed
- ~ 2 tablespoons olive oil
- ~ 1/3 cup balsamic vinegar
- ~ 1 pound bay scallops
- ~ 1 (10-ounce) package frozen spinach
- ~ 8 ounces uncooked pappardelle

Combine the sun-dried tomatoes, lemon juice, 1/4 cup olive oil, cheese, salt and pepper in a pasta bowl; set aside. Sauté the garlic in 2 table-spoons olive oil in a medium skillet over medium heat. Add the vinegar and scallops. Cook for 5 minutes, shaking the skillet occasionally. Cook the spinach using the package directions. Add the scallops and spinach to the tomato mixture and mix gently; keep warm. Cook the pasta for 7 minutes or until al dente; drain. Add to the scallop mixture and toss to mix. Yields 2 servings.

Seafood

"**Progress in
civilization has been
accompanied by
progress in cookery.**"
—**Fannie Farmer**

Lasagna Baia Bianca

This recipe comes from Fabrizio Iannucci of Il Piccolo and Pizzico Restaurants. He recommends a Mastroberardino Vignadangelo, 1992, from Campania.

- ~ Olive oil
- ~ Salt to taste
- ~ 4 (8x10-inch) sheets of fresh pasta
- ~ 16 ounces bay scallops
- ~ 4 ounces brandy
- ~ 1/4 cup unsalted butter

- ~ 1/4 cup flour
- ~ 4 cups half-and-half or light cream
- ~ 1 small sweet red onion, coarsely chopped
- ~ 2 teaspoons lobster base (optional)

- ~ White pepper to taste
- ~ 15 basil leaves, chopped
- ~ 6 thin slices mozzarella cheese, cut into squares
- ~ 1 cup grated Parmesan cheese

Add a drop of olive oil to salted boiling water in a large stockpot and add the pasta. Cook for 4 minutes; rinse in cold water and drain. Lay pasta out on a towel. Sauté the scallops in the brandy and half the butter in a saucepan for 3 minutes; drain, reserving the pan juices. Melt the remaining butter in a heavy saucepan and blend in the flour. Cook for several minutes over very low heat. Combine the half-and-half, the reserved pan juices, onion, lobster base and white pepper in a saucepan. Bring to a boil and stir in the butter and flour mixture. Cook over low heat for 2 to 3 minutes or until thickened, stirring constantly. Strain through a fine sieve into a bowl and stir in the basil. Spread a small amount of the sauce in a shallow baking dish. Alternate layers of the pasta, scallops, mozzarella cheese, Parmesan cheese and remaining
sauce in the prepared baking dish until all the ingredients are used. Bake at 300 degrees for 45 minutes. Yields 6 servings.

130

Fettuccini with Grilled Shrimp in Oyster Brie Sauce

Rue de l'espoir gives us this seafood dish which is good with pasta or rice. Serve it with a Santa Margherita Pinot Grigio, 1993, or a Sancerre (Chavignol), 1991.

- ~ 2 ounces finely chopped onions
- ~ 2 ounces finely chopped carrots
- ~ 2 ounces finely chopped celery
- ~ 1/2 cup butter
- ~ 1 cup flour
- ~ 2 cups heavy cream, scalded

- ~ 1 cup oyster liquid, clam juice or fish stock
- ~ 4 ounces Brie cheese, rind trimmed, cubed
- ~ 2 red bell peppers, roasted, peeled, seeded, chopped
- ~ Lemon juice
- ~ Salt and pepper to taste

- ~ 1/2 to 1 pint oysters, in liquid
- ~ 16 ounces fettuccini, cooked
- ~ 16 jumbo shrimp, peeled
- ~ 2 cloves of garlic
- ~ 4 ounces clarified butter
- ~ Lemon wedges
- ~ Chopped parsley

Sauté the onion, carrots and celery in 1/2 cup butter in a saucepan until the onion is translucent. Stir in the flour until the vegetables are well coated. Stir in the cream and cook until thickened. Add the seafood liquid and cheese. Cook over low heat until the cheese melts. Add the bell peppers, lemon juice, salt and pepper; keep warm. Poach the oysters in their own liquid in a saucepan just until the edges are slightly curled; remove from the liquid and keep warm. Toss the pasta in a serving bowl with a small amount of the sauce and thin with the remaining oyster liquid if desired. Grill the shrimp with the garlic and clarified butter until opaque. Pour the remaining sauce over the pasta and then arrange the oysters and shrimp to cover the pasta. Garnish with lemon wedges and chopped parsley. Yields 4 servings.

Warren, settled on
the Kickemuit River
in 1653, became a
prosperous whaling
and shipbuilding
community. Indians
taught the colonists
to gather quahogs,
scallops and oysters,
delicacies enjoyed
throughout the
world. Oystering
became Rhode
Island's third
largest industry in
the 19th century.
These naturally
occurring shellfish
were intentionally
seeded in over
25,000 acres of
oyster beds in
Narragansett Bay.
Warren was the site

Spaghetti with Shrimp Sauce

Serve with grated Parmesan cheese and Westport Rivers Chardonnay.

~ 1 small onion,
  chopped
~ 3 tablespoons olive
  oil
~ 1 pound shrimp,
  peeled
~ 1/3 cup dry white
  wine

~ 10 ounces fresh or
  canned plum
  tomatoes, peeled,
  chopped
~ Salt and freshly
  ground pepper
  to taste

~ 1 tablespoon
  chopped flat-leaf
  parsley
~ 16 ounces uncooked
  spaghetti

Boil water in a large stockpot for pasta. Sauté the onion in the heated
olive oil in a large skillet over low heat for 3 minutes or until translucent.
Add the peeled shrimp and increase the heat to medium. Sauté for 2
minutes. Stir in the wine. Cook for 2 minutes more or until the wine
evaporates. Stir in the tomatoes, salt and pepper. Cook for 2 minutes. Add
the parsley. Cook for 2 minutes longer; keep warm. Cook the pasta
al dente; drain. Spoon onto a warm serving platter and spoon the shrimp
sauce over the top. Yields 4 servings.

Newport Seafood and Rice Casserole

Dazzle your guests with this easy and elegant dish. Serve it with a
Muscadet De Sevre et Maine, 1990, or a Stag's Leap Chardonnay, 1992.

~ 1 cup chopped celery
~ 1 cup chopped onion
~ 1 medium green bell
  pepper, chopped
~ 1 tablespoon butter
~ 2 tablespoons olive
  oil
~ 1 cup uncooked rice

~ 1 can chicken broth
~ 1 cup water
~ 8 ounces
  mushrooms, sliced
~ 1 pound medium to
  large shrimp, peeled
~ 8 ounces crab meat,
  cooked

~ 8 ounces uncooked
  scallops
~ 8 ounces lobster
  meat
~ 1 cup mayonnaise
~ 1 teaspoon curry
  powder

Sauté the celery, onion and green pepper in the butter and olive oil
in a skillet until tender. Cook the rice in the chicken broth and water in
a saucepan until tender. Combine the sautéed vegetables, rice and
remaining ingredients in a bowl and mix well. Spoon into a 2- or 3-quart
baking dish. Bake at 350 degrees for 45 minutes. Yields 6 to 8 servings.

of many of the state's major shucking and packing houses, shipping thousands of gallons of opened oysters each day. Unfortunately, the oyster beds were destroyed by hurricanes and pollution, and the industry ended in the 1950s.

Hot Barbecued Shrimp

Serve barbecued shrimp in deep bowls with warm bread for soaking up the sauce.

- ~ 3 pounds large or jumbo unpeeled shrimp
- ~ 3/4 cup butter, sliced
- ~ 1/2 cup olive oil
- ~ 3/4 cup dry white wine
- ~ 1/4 cup Worcestershire sauce
- ~ 2 to 3 teaspoons Tabasco sauce
- ~ 1/3 cup chopped parsley
- ~ 1/4 cup chopped garlic
- ~ 1 tablespoon dried rosemary
- ~ 1 to 2 teaspoons cayenne pepper
- ~ 1 lemon, thinly sliced

Place the shrimp in a deep Dutch oven or baking dish. Top with the sliced butter. Combine the olive oil, wine, Worcestershire sauce, Tabasco sauce, parsley, garlic, rosemary and cayenne pepper in a bowl and mix well. Pour over the shrimp. Top with the lemon slices. Bake at 350 degrees for 30 minutes or until the shrimp are pink. Yields 8 servings.

Grilled Sweet and Tart Shrimp

This also makes a delightful appetizer, served with wooden skewers.

- ~ 2 tablespoons coarse-grain Dijon mustard
- ~ 2 tablespoons white wine vinegar
- ~ 2 tablespoons vegetable oil
- ~ 2 tablespoons honey
- ~ 1 1/4 pounds extra-large shrimp
- ~ Orange and lime wedges

Combine the mustard, vinegar, oil and honey in a shallow dish and mix well. Peel and devein the shrimp, leaving the tails intact. Add to the marinade and toss to coat well. Marinate, covered, in the refrigerator for one to two hours, stirring occasionally. Drain, reserving the marinade. Grill the shrimp over hot coals for 3 to 5 minutes or until cooked through, turning once and basting with the marinade frequently. Serve warm, garnished with orange and lime wedges. Yields 4 servings.

Seafood Paella

Paella is a very flexible dish. A little saffron, a lot of rice and varying amounts of whatever seafood is fresh and available are all that is needed for an incomparable meal.

- ~ 5 cups chicken broth
- ~ 1/2 cup dry white wine
- ~ 1 bay leaf
- ~ 1/4 teaspoon saffron thread
- ~ 1 red or yellow bell pepper, chopped
- ~ 6 tablespoons olive oil
- ~ 1 medium onion, chopped
- ~ 5 cloves of garlic, minced
- ~ 2 medium tomatoes, peeled, seeded, chopped
- ~ 1 tablespoon minced parsley
- ~ 2 1/2 cups uncooked arborio or other short grain rice
- ~ 4 links smoked salmon sausage, chopped
- ~ 8 ounces medium shrimp
- ~ 1 1/4 pounds cooked lobster or crab meat
- ~ 18 small mussels, scrubbed, debearded
- ~ 1/2 cup fresh or frozen peas
- ~ Salt and pepper to taste

Bring the chicken broth, wine, bay leaf and saffron to a simmer in a small saucepan. Sauté the bell pepper in the heated olive oil in a paella pan for 3 minutes. Add the onion, garlic, tomatoes and parsley. Cook for 2 minutes. Stir in the rice and broth mixture. Cook over medium-high heat for 5 to 10 minutes. Reduce the heat to low and cook for 10 minutes longer. Stir in the sausage and shrimp. Add the lobster, mussels and peas. Let stand, loosely covered, for 5 to 10 minutes or until the seafood is cooked through. Season with salt and pepper to taste.
Yields 6 servings.

A Tasteful

Reflection of

Historic

Rhode Island

Complements

Vegetables

Polenta and Rice

Pasta

Asparagus Mimosa

~ 1 teaspoon butter
~ 2 tablespoons dry bread crumbs
~ 1 hard-cooked egg white

~ 1/2 teaspoon salt
~ 1 pound asparagus, trimmed
~ 1 tablespoon butter

~ Several drops of lemon juice
~ 1/8 teaspoon salt
~ Freshly ground pepper to taste

Heat one teaspoon butter until foamy in a nonstick 8-inch skillet sprayed with nonstick cooking spray. Add the bread crumbs. Sauté until light brown and remove from the heat. Sieve the egg white into the bread crumbs and mix gently. Remove to a piece of waxed paper. Fill a 12-inch or larger skillet 3/4 full with water. Add 1/2 teaspoon salt and asparagus. Cook for 6 to 8 minutes or until crisp-tender. Remove to a serving bowl. Melt 1 tablespoon butter with the lemon juice in the skillet. Drizzle over the asparagus and sprinkle with 1/8 teaspoon salt, pepper and the crumb mixture. Yields 4 servings.

Boston Baked Beans

Every cook in New England has a version of this regional favorite.

~ 16 ounces dried navy or pea beans
~ 6 cups water
~ 1/2 teaspoon baking soda

~ 8 ounces salt pork, cut into 1/2-inch pieces
~ 1 small onion, chopped

~ 1/3 cup molasses
~ 1/4 cup sugar
~ 1 teaspoon dry mustard
~ 1/4 teaspoon pepper

Soak the beans in the water in a large bowl for 8 hours or longer. Combine undrained beans with the baking soda in a large saucepan. Bring to a boil and reduce the heat. Cook for 10 minutes. Drain, reserving the liquid. Combine the beans with the salt pork and onion in a 2-quart bean pot or baking dish. Combine the molasses, sugar, dry mustard, pepper and one cup of the reserved bean liquid in a bowl. Pour over the beans and mix well. Add about one cup reserved liquid or just enough to cover the beans. Bake, covered, at 300 degrees for 2 hours. Add one cup reserved liquid and mix well. Bake for 1 1/2 to 2 hours longer or until the beans are tender and the liquid is absorbed, removing the cover during the last 30 minutes. Yields 8 servings.

The village of Chepachet, in Glocester, is home to the Brown and Hopkins Country Store, reportedly the oldest country store in continuous operation in America. The building was originally a millinery when it was opened in 1799. Revolutionary War veteran Ira Evans purchased the building in 1809 and opened a general store there filled with every conceivable item, from hogsheads of molasses to barrels

Easy Black Beans and Yellow Rice

This dish goes well with pork, but it is hearty enough for a warming meal on a cold night.

~ 1/2 cup chopped onion
~ 1/4 cup chopped celery
~ 1/4 cup chopped green bell pepper
~ 2 cloves of garlic, minced
~ 1 (16-ounce) can black beans

~ 1 (15-ounce) can whole tomatoes, chopped
~ 1 teaspoon sugar
~ 3/4 teaspoon Italian seasoning
~ 1/8 teaspoon Tabasco sauce
~ 3/4 cup water
~ 1/8 teaspoon salt

~ 1/4 teaspoon pepper
~ 3/4 cup water
~ 1/3 cup uncooked rice
~ 1/4 teaspoon turmeric

Sauté the onion, celery, green pepper and garlic until tender in a heated electric skillet sprayed with nonstick cooking spray. Add the beans, tomatoes, sugar, Italian seasoning, Tabasco, 3/4 cup water, salt and pepper and mix well. Bring to a boil and reduce the heat. Simmer for 15 minutes or until thickened, stirring occasionally. Bring 3/4 cup water, rice and turmeric to a boil in a saucepan. Reduce the heat and simmer, covered, for 20 minutes. Remove from the heat and let stand, covered, for 5 minutes or until the liquid is absorbed. Spoon onto serving plates and spoon the beans over the top. Yields 2 to 4 servings.

Complements

of flour and sacks of feed. Although the store has changed hands many times since 1809, it has remained open, often serving as both a social and political center for the community. Today, this authentic country store, complete with potbellied stove, sells gourmet foods, handcrafts, and antiques.

Creamy Broccoli and Zucchini

This is hearty enough to serve as a main dish, with a salad and bread.

~ 2 cups chopped fresh broccoli
~ 2 cups chopped unpeeled zucchini
~ 1/2 cup chopped onion
~ 1 clove of garlic, minced

~ 2 tablespoons butter
~ 3 tablespoons flour
~ 2 tablespoons chopped parsley
~ 1/2 teaspoon oregano
~ 1/2 teaspoon salt
~ White pepper to taste

~ 3/4 cup milk
~ 1 1/2 cups ricotta cheese or part skim milk ricotta cheese
~ 8 ounces spinach noodles, cooked, drained

Cook the broccoli and zucchini in a small amount of water in a saucepan for 8 to 10 minutes or until tender. Sauté the onion and garlic in butter in a large saucepan until the onion is tender. Stir in the flour, parsley, oregano, salt and white pepper. Stir in the milk. Cook until thickened, stirring constantly. Stir in the ricotta cheese. Cook until the cheese is nearly melted. Add the sautéed vegetables. Cook until heated through. Thin the mixture with low-fat milk if necessary for the desired consistency. Serve over the noodles. Pass Parmesan cheese to sprinkle over servings. Yields 4 to 6 servings.

Sesame Broccoli

This is certainly not the "same old broccoli" and it is quick and easy to do.

~ Florets of 1 large bunch broccoli
~ 1/2 cup toasted sesame seeds

~ 1 1/2 tablespoons soy sauce

~ 2 tablespoons hot sesame oil
~ 2 teaspoons honey

Steam the broccoli over boiling water until tender. Cool to room temperature. Combine half the sesame seeds, soy sauce, sesame oil and honey in a bowl and mix well. Arrange the broccoli on a serving platter. Drizzle with the sesame mixture and sprinkle with the remaining sesame seeds. Serve at room temperature. Yields 4 to 6 servings.

**Johnston,
established in 1636,
is the location of
the historic Dame
Farm, a 500-acre
working farm that
dates from the late
18th century. The
site, an excellent
example of colonial
agriculture, has the
rich soil utilized by
early settlers for
pastures and for
growing such crops
as corn, oats, barley,
buckwheat and
potatoes. Fruit
cultivation,
particularly that
of apples, also was
common in the
area, which is also
known for its apple**

Red Cabbage with Apples

The tart taste of Granny Smith apples adds a special zip to the cabbage in this dish.

~ 1 (2-pound) head red cabbage, shredded
~ 2 tart apples, peeled, shredded
~ 1/3 cup white wine vinegar
~ 1 1/2 cups boiling water
~ 4 whole cloves
~ 1 teaspoon salt
~ 2 tablespoons butter
~ 1 1/2 tablespoons sugar
~ Chopped parsley

Combine the cabbage, apples, vinegar, boiling water, cloves and salt in a large heavy saucepan. Bring to a boil and reduce the heat. Simmer for one hour, stirring occasionally. Stir in the butter and sugar. Simmer until most of the liquid has evaporated, stirring occasionally. Sprinkle with the parsley. Yields 6 to 8 servings.

Glazed Carrots and Shallots

Serve this colorful dish with Salmon in Red Wine Sauce (page 118).

~ 1 pound baby carrots, peeled
~ 8 shallots
~ 3 tablespoons unsalted butter
~ 2 tablespoons sugar
~ 2 tablespoons water
~ Salt and pepper to taste
~ Minced fresh parsley

Blanch the carrots and shallots in boiling water in a saucepan for one minute. Drain and immerse in ice water; drain again. Bring the butter, sugar and water to a boil in a large heavy saucepan over medium heat. Add the vegetables and mix well. Season with salt and pepper. Cook, covered, for 20 minutes or until the vegetables are tender, stirring occasionally. Top the servings with parsley. Yields 6 servings.

cider production.
Native Americans
taught the colonists
to raise foods
indigenous to the
area such as
pumpkins, squash,
beans, sweet
potatoes and a
variety of berries.
One of the first
recipes learned was
for succotash, a
mixture of corn
and beans.

Carrots and Pea Pods in Orange Sauce

Add visual excitement to any entrée with this colorful dish. The secret is not to overcook the vegetables. You may substitute frozen pea pods for the fresh ones.

- ~ 1 cup diagonally sliced carrots
- ~ Salt to taste
- ~ 2 cups fresh pea pods
- ~ 1/3 cup orange juice
- ~ 1 teaspoon cornstarch
- ~ 1/2 teaspoon finely grated orange zest
- ~ 2 teaspoons soy sauce

Cook the carrots, covered, in a small amount of salted boiling water in a medium saucepan for 5 minutes. Add the pea pods. Cook for 2 to 4 minutes longer or until the vegetables are tender-crisp; drain and keep warm in the covered saucepan. Blend the orange juice and cornstarch in a small saucepan. Cook over medium heat until thickened, stirring constantly. Cook for 2 minutes longer, stirring constantly. Stir in the orange zest and soy sauce. Toss with the vegetables in a serving bowl. Yields 6 servings.

Carrot Soufflé

This is a nice addition to a holiday dinner. Even those who don't like carrots will enjoy this.

- ~ 2 cups mashed cooked carrots
- ~ 1/2 cup butter, softened
- ~ 1 cup sugar
- ~ 3 eggs
- ~ 1 tablespoon flour
- ~ 1 teaspoon baking powder
- ~ 1 cup milk
- ~ 1/4 teaspoon cinnamon
- ~ 1 teaspoon salt

Combine the carrots, butter, sugar, eggs, flour, baking powder, milk, cinnamon and salt in a bowl and mix well. Spoon into a 2-quart baking dish. Bake at 350 degrees for 45 minutes. Yields 8 servings.

Chick-Peas in Tangy Tamarind Sauce

Serve this Indian dish with basmati rice, puffy deep-fried Indian bread and Sakonnet Gewürztraminer for a vegetarian meal.

~ 1 (1 1/2-inch) ball tamarind pulp or 1 teaspoon tamarind paste
~ 1 1/2 cups boiling water
~ 1 1/2 cups thinly sliced onions
~ 1/2 cup light vegetable oil
~ 2 teaspoons minced garlic

~ 1/2 teaspoon turmeric
~ 1/2 teaspoon red chile pepper or cayenne pepper to taste
~ 1 cup fresh or canned tomato, chopped
~ 1 tablespoon grated fresh ginger

~ 2 (20-ounce) cans chick-peas
~ 1 1/2 teaspoons garam masala
~ 1 1/4 teaspoons roasted ground cumin seeds
~ Salt to taste
~ Sliced onions
~ Red chile peppers

Soak the tamarind pulp in the boiling water in a small bowl for 15 minutes. Mash as much of the liquid as possible from the pulp and strain into a small bowl, discarding the fibrous residue. Caramelize the onions in the heated oil in a large heavy-bottomed saucepan over medium-high heat for 20 minutes, stirring constantly; do not over-brown. Add the garlic. Cook for 2 minutes. Add the turmeric and red pepper. Cook for one minute, stirring constantly. Stir in the tomato and ginger. Reduce the heat to medium and cook for 5 minutes or until the oil begins to separate from the mixture. Drain the chick-peas, reserving one cup liquid. Stir the reserved chick-pea liquid and tamarind into the onion mixture. Simmer, covered, for 15 minutes. Stir in the chick-peas, garam masala and cumin. Cook for 10 minutes. Season with salt. Garnish with onions and chiles. Yields 8 to 12 servings.

Baked Fennel and Gorgonzola

Serve something a little different with this easy vegetable dish.

- ~ 4 (3 1/2-inch wide) fennel heads with greens
- ~ 1 3/4 cups reduced-sodium chicken stock
- ~ 4 ounces Gorgonzola cheese
- ~ 2 tablespoons fine dry bread crumbs
- ~ Pepper to taste
- ~ Chopped parsley

Chop and reserve one cup of the fennel greens. Cut the bulbs into halves. Arrange the bulbs in a 10- to 12-inch skillet and add the chicken stock. Cover and bring to a boil over high heat; reduce the heat. Simmer for 20 to 25 minutes or until tender. Remove to a 9- or 10-inch baking dish with a slotted spoon. Cook the chicken stock until reduced to 1/3 cup. Stir in the fennel greens. Spoon over the fennel in the baking dish. Mash the cheese with the bread crumbs in a bowl. Spoon over the casserole. Bake at 375 degrees for 20 minutes or until the casserole is heated through and the cheese begins to brown. Season with the pepper and sprinkle with parsley. Yields 8 servings.

Potato and Artichoke Gratin

The flavors of the potatoes and artichokes make an interesting combination and are a delicious accompaniment to chicken or lamb.

- ~ 3 potatoes, thinly sliced
- ~ 1 cup water
- ~ 5 fresh artichoke hearts, thinly sliced
- ~ 3/4 cup evaporated skim milk
- ~ 1 1/2 cups skim milk
- ~ 2 ounces goat cheese, crumbled
- ~ 1 teaspoon minced fresh tarragon
- ~ Nutmeg and pepper to taste
- ~ 1 teaspoon salt
- ~ 2 tablespoons bread crumbs
- ~ 1 tablespoon grated Parmesan cheese

Combine the potatoes with the water in a microwave-safe dish. Microwave on High for 8 minutes; drain. Layer the artichokes and potatoes 1/2 at a time in a buttered 8x10-inch baking dish, arranging the top layer in overlapping rows. Combine the evaporated skim milk and skim milk in a bowl and mix well. Pour over the layers. Top with the goat cheese, tarragon, nutmeg, pepper and salt. Sprinkle with the bread crumbs and Parmesan cheese. Bake at 425 degrees in the upper third of the oven for 30 minutes or until bubbly and brown. Yields 4 to 6 servings.

For over 200 years, the annual Civic, Military and Fireman's Parade in Bristol has celebrated our nation's Declaration of Independence on the Fourth of July. Attracting nearly a quarter of a million visitors and heritage groups from all over the world, this old-fashioned parade is a triumph of marching bands, antique cars, floats, clowns and military units in uniforms dating from the Revolution to the present.

Baked Cheese Potatoes

This is a tasty comfort dish that is also low in fat. It goes well with beef and poultry.

~ 3 pounds unpeeled Yukon Gold or russet potatoes
~ 6 cloves of garlic
~ 1 1/2 cups low-fat cottage cheese
~ 1/2 cup light sour cream
~ 1 1/2 teaspoons salt
~ 1/4 teaspoon freshly ground pepper
~ 1 bunch scallions, sliced
~ 1/2 cup shredded extra-sharp Cheddar cheese
~ 1/4 teaspoon paprika

Combine the potatoes and garlic with cold water to cover in a large saucepan. Simmer for 15 to 20 minutes or until the potatoes are tender. Drain and cool for 20 minutes. Peel and grate the potatoes or shred in a food processor; set aside. Process the garlic and cottage cheese in the food processor until smooth. Add the sour cream, salt and pepper and process until well mixed. Process with the potatoes and scallions in a bowl and mix well. Spoon into a 2-quart baking dish lightly coated with nonstick cooking spray. Top with the cheese and paprika. Bake at 350 degrees for 30 to 40 minutes or until heated through. Yields 8 servings.

Garlic and Rosemary Mashed Potatoes

~ 3 3/4 pounds red potatoes, peeled, cut into 1-inch pieces
~ 9 large cloves of garlic
~ Salt to taste
~ 2 tablespoons butter
~ 2 tablespoons chopped fresh rosemary or 2 teaspoons dried rosemary
~ 1/2 cup (or more) chicken broth
~ 1/2 cup grated Parmesan cheese
~ Pepper to taste
~ Fresh sprigs of rosemary

Cook the potatoes and garlic in salted boiling water in a saucepan for 30 minutes or until very tender; drain. Transfer to a large mixing bowl and beat until smooth. Beat in the butter and chopped rosemary. Bring the chicken broth to a simmer in a saucepan. Add to the potatoes gradually, beating constantly until smooth. Stir in the cheese, salt and pepper. Spoon into a serving bowl and garnish with rosemary sprigs. Yields 8 servings.

Lemon and Chive Potatoes

Judy Rush of the International Gourmet Society, who shares this recipe, recommends serving it with grilled or broiled chicken.

~ 1 1/2 pounds new potatoes
~ 1/4 cup butter
~ 1 teaspoon grated lemon rind

~ 2 tablespoons lemon juice
~ 4 teaspoons chopped chives

~ Nutmeg to taste
~ 1 teaspoon salt
~ 1/4 teaspoon pepper

Cook the potatoes in water to cover in a saucepan until tender; drain and keep warm. Combine the butter, lemon rind, lemon juice, chives, nutmeg, salt and pepper in a saucepan. Cook until the butter melts, stirring to mix well. Add the potatoes and mix gently. Cook just until heated through. Yields 4 servings.

Scalloped Potatoes with Leeks and Cream

Try this for a different accompaniment to steak or chicken.

~ 1/4 cup unsalted butter
~ 4 cups sliced leeks, white and pale green parts only
~ Salt and pepper to taste

~ 2 cups whipping cream
~ 3 large cloves of garlic, minced
~ 4 pounds russet potatoes, peeled, thinly sliced

~ 2 cups shredded white Cheddar cheese or Gruyère cheese
~ 1/3 cup freshly grated Parmesan cheese

Melt the butter in a large heavy skillet over medium-high heat. Add the leeks, stirring to coat well. Reduce the heat to medium-low. Cook, covered, for 8 minutes or until the leeks are tender, stirring occasionally. Cook, uncovered, for 3 minutes or until most of the liquid has evaporated. Season with salt and pepper. Mix the cream and garlic in a small bowl. Layer the potatoes, leeks, Cheddar cheese and cream mixture 1/2 at a time in a buttered 9x13-inch baking dish, sprinkling the potatoes with salt and pepper. Top with the Parmesan cheese. Chill, covered, for up to 6 hours. Let stand at room temperature for one hour. Bake at 375 degrees for 1 1/4 hours. Let stand for 15 minutes before serving. Yields 8 servings.

Foster was a farming community in the colonial era. While many crops were grown and harvested, corn was one of the area's staples. The job of husking ripened corn was a very large one. It was common during harvest time to hold a husking bee, where young men and women from miles around gathered to husk the corn in a barn amidst much merrymaking. If a man found a red ear of corn, he gave all the girls a kiss. If a young woman found

Butternut Squash with Onions and Pecans

This is definitely not your mother's butternut squash recipe!

~ 1 medium to large onion, finely chopped
~ 1/4 cup butter

~ 5 cups chopped butternut squash
~ Salt and pepper to taste

~ 3/4 cup coarsely chopped pecans
~ 3 tablespoons minced fresh parsley

Sauté the onion in the butter in a large skillet over low heat for 10 to 12 minutes or until very translucent. Add the squash, tossing to coat well. Cook, covered, for 15 minutes or until the squash is tender but still holds its shape, stirring frequently with a wooden spoon. Season with salt and pepper. Stir in half the pecans and parsley. Spoon into a serving bowl and sprinkle with the remaining pecans and parsley. Yields 6 servings.

Sweet Potato and Carrot Purée

Make crème fraîche by combining one teaspoon of buttermilk with one cup of whipping cream and heating to just under 85 degrees. Let stand, loosely covered, at 60 to 85 degrees until it thickens. Stir, cover and store in the refrigerator until needed.

~ 4 (8-ounce) sweet potatoes
~ 1 pound carrots, peeled
~ 2 1/2 cups water

~ 1 tablespoon sugar
~ 3/4 cup unsalted butter, softened
~ Salt and pepper to taste

~ 1/2 cup crème fraîche
~ 1/2 teaspoon freshly grated nutmeg
~ Cayenne pepper to taste

Pierce each potato with a knife and place on the center oven rack. Bake at 375 degrees for one hour or until tender when pierced with a fork. Cut the carrots into one-inch pieces and combine with the water, sugar, 2 tablespoons of the butter, salt and pepper in a saucepan. Cook over medium heat for 30 minutes or until the water has evaporated and the carrots begin to sizzle in the butter. Add additional water and cook longer if the carrots are not tender. Scoop out the sweet potato pulp and combine with the carrots in a food processor. Add the remaining butter and crème fraîche and process until very smooth. Add the nutmeg, salt, cayenne pepper and pepper and mix briefly. Serve immediately or reheat in a covered baking dish at 350 degrees for 25 minutes. Yields 6 servings.

a red ear, she kissed the man of her choice. When the cornhusking was done, a supper was served along with sweet cider and followed by dancing and games.

Zucchini Soufflé

Zucchini is available throughout the year and this soufflé is a nice light accompaniment to any entrée or brunch.

- ~ 1 clove of garlic
- ~ 1 large onion
- ~ 3 cups grated zucchini
- ~ 4 eggs
- ~ 1/2 cup vegetable oil or olive oil
- ~ 2 teaspoons Italian seasoning
- ~ 1 teaspoon salt
- ~ Pepper to taste
- ~ 1 cup baking mix
- ~ 1 cup grated Parmesan cheese

Chop the garlic and onion in a food processor. Combine with the zucchini in a bowl. Beat the eggs and oil in a mixing bowl until smooth. Add to the zucchini mixture with the Italian seasoning, salt, pepper, baking mix and half the cheese and mix well. Spoon into a gratin dish and sprinkle with the remaining cheese. Bake at 350 degrees for 45 to 50 minutes or until the soufflé is set and the top is brown. Yields 8 servings.

Papaya and Red Pepper Relish

This relish is a wonderful complement to grilled or roasted meat, poultry or seafood. It can be prepared with mangoes as well as papayas.

- ~ 3 cups cider vinegar
- ~ 1 cup sugar
- ~ 2 yellow onions, thinly sliced
- ~ 1 1/2 teaspoons salt
- ~ 6 red bell peppers, roasted, peeled, sliced
- ~ 2 jalapeño peppers, seeded, minced
- ~ 2 fresh papayas, cut into strips
- ~ Freshly ground pepper to taste

Bring the vinegar and sugar to a boil in a 2-quart saucepan. Add the onions and salt. Remove from the heat and let stand for 15 minutes. Add the bell peppers and jalapeño peppers. Place in a bowl and chill in the refrigerator. Drain just before serving, add the papayas and season with pepper. Yields 4 cups.

Complements

**"A good cook is
like a sorceress
who dispenses
happiness."
—Elsa Schiaparelli**

Grilled Vegetable Salsa

The ingredients for this salsa can be varied to suit your individual tastes,
but the results are always delicious. Serve it with Marinated London Broil
(page 87) or poultry.

- 8 (1-ounce) baby
  artichokes or 1 cup
  drained canned
  artichoke hearts
- 4 medium tomatoes
- 1 red or yellow bell
  pepper
- 1 medium red or
  yellow onion
- Olive oil for
  brushing

- 25 niçoise or
  kalamata olives, cut
  into quarters
- 1/4 cup drained
  capers
- 1/4 cup fruity
  extra-virgin olive oil
- 2 tablespoons fresh
  lemon juice
- 1 cup chopped fresh
  basil

- 1/2 cup finely
  chopped flat-leaf
  parsley
- Salt, cayenne pepper
  and freshly ground
  black pepper to taste

Brush the artichokes, tomatoes, bell pepper, onion and grill with oil.
Sear the vegetables on a hot grill for one minute and then move to a
cooler area of grill. Grill just until tender, turning frequently and
brushing with additional oil if necessary. Cool the vegetables. Slice the
artichoke hearts, peel and slice the tomatoes and pepper and chop the
onion. Combine with the olives, capers, 1/4 cup olive oil, lemon juice,
basil, parsley, salt, cayenne pepper and black pepper in a bowl and mix
well. Serve warm or at room temperature. Yields 3 cups.

Marinades for Grilled Vegetables

Grilling is not just a way to prepare food fast without a lot of fuss, it is also a way to impart special flavor to food with the help of these easy marinades.

Vinegar and Oil Marinade:
- ~ 1/2 cup vegetable oil
- ~ 1/2 cup red wine vinegar
- ~ 1 teaspoon minced garlic
- ~ 1 tablespoon dried basil
- ~ 1 teaspoon dried oregano
- ~ 2 teaspoons kosher salt
- ~ 1 teaspoon pepper

Champagne and Mustard Vinaigrette:
- ~ 2 tablespoons Champagne vinegar
- ~ 1 teaspoon Dijon mustard
- ~ 1/3 cup olive oil
- ~ 1/4 cup chopped fresh basil leaves
- ~ 1 clove of garlic, minced
- ~ 1 teaspoon salt
- ~ 1/2 teaspoon pepper

Combine the ingredients for the marinade in a bowl and mix well. Use to brush on sliced or bite-size vegetables before grilling until tender and golden brown on both sides; remove to a serving platter as they become tender. Drizzle with the remaining marinade. Yields variable amounts.

Spicy Black Bean and Corn Salsa

This is especially good with Grilled Salmon Sandwich with Mustard Sauce (page 122). If you make it in advance, add the tomato at serving time. Add minced jalapeño pepper for a zippier taste.

- ~ 2 cups drained canned black beans
- ~ 8 ounces steamed fresh corn or canned corn
- ~ 1/2 cup chopped cilantro
- ~ 1/4 cup each minced red and green onion
- ~ 6 tablespoons fresh lime juice
- ~ 6 tablespoons vegetable oil
- ~ 1 1/2 teaspoons ground cumin
- ~ Salt and pepper to taste
- ~ 1/2 cup chopped tomato

Combine the beans, corn, cilantro, red onion, green onion, lime juice and vegetable oil in a bowl. Stir in the cumin, salt and pepper. Chill until serving time. Add the tomato just before serving. Yields 4 cups.

Complements

Herbed Polenta

Thanks to Chefs Greg Maser and Michael Bradley of Hospital Trust Bank for this Italian classic.

~ 7 cups light chicken stock
~ 1 1/2 cups coarse-ground cornmeal
~ 1/4 teaspoon salt
~ 1 teaspoon finely chopped fresh thyme
~ 1 teaspoon finely chopped fresh basil
~ 1 teaspoon finely chopped fresh oregano
~ Lightly salted butter for frying

Bring the chicken stock to a boil in a saucepan. Add the cornmeal very gradually, whisking constantly. Stir in the salt, thyme, basil and oregano. Simmer until the mixture pulls from the side of the pan. Pour into a buttered loaf pan. Let stand until set. Invert onto a work surface and cut into slices. Fry in the butter in a skillet until the edges are slightly crisp. Yields 6 servings.

Lemon Pilaf with Currants and Almonds

Lemon Pilaf is a savory crunchy accompaniment to fish and lamb and a natural with veal curry.

~ 1 tablespoon minced onion
~ 1 tablespoon unsalted butter
~ 1 cup long grain white rice
~ 1 1/2 cups seasoned chicken broth
~ 1/4 cup lemon juice
~ Finely minced zest of 1 lemon
~ 2 tablespoons currants
~ 1 tablespoon unsalted butter
~ 1/4 cup lightly toasted slivered almonds

Sauté the onion in 1 tablespoon butter in a 2-quart saucepan until tender. Add the rice and stir to coat well. Stir in the chicken broth, lemon juice, lemon zest and currants. Bring to a boil. Reduce the heat and simmer, covered, for 20 minutes or until the liquid is absorbed and the rice is tender. Add one tablespoon butter and the almonds and mix lightly. Serve immediately. Yields 4 to 6 servings.

Risotto with Asparagus and Pine Nuts

Arborio rice is a good choice for this Italian dish. Japanese rice is also a good alternative.

- ~ 1 pound fresh asparagus
- ~ 1 shallot, minced
- ~ 2 tablespoons butter
- ~ 8 ounces uncooked long grain rice
- ~ 1/2 cup dry white wine
- ~ 2 to 3 cups chicken broth
- ~ 6 tablespoons freshly grated Parmesan cheese
- ~ 3/4 cup whipping cream
- ~ 2 cloves of garlic, minced
- ~ Salt to taste
- ~ 1/2 teaspoon pepper
- ~ 1/2 cup toasted pine nuts

Cut off the asparagus tips and set aside. Slice the stems. Sauté the shallot in the butter in a saucepan until golden brown. Stir in the rice. Add the wine and cook until the wine is absorbed, stirring constantly. Add the asparagus stems. Stir in the broth 1/2 cup at a time, cooking until the liquid is absorbed after each addition and stirring constantly. Add the cheese, cream, garlic, salt and pepper and mix well. Stir in the asparagus tips and pine nuts and remove from the heat. Let stand for 5 minutes before serving. Yields 6 to 8 servings.

Saffron Rice

This rice dish is particularly good with fish.

- ~ 1 cup uncooked long grain rice
- ~ 1/2 cup finely chopped onion
- ~ 1/4 cup butter
- ~ 3/4 cup dry white wine
- ~ 1 cup chicken broth
- ~ 1/8 teaspoon saffron
- ~ 1/4 cup butter
- ~ 2 ounces Parmesan cheese, grated

Sauté the rice and onion in 1/4 cup butter in a heavy saucepan over low heat until the onion is translucent. Add the wine and chicken broth. Bring to a boil and stir in the saffron. Reduce the heat and cover the saucepan. Simmer for 30 minutes or until the liquid is absorbed and the rice is tender. Stir in 1/4 cup butter and the Parmesan cheese.
Yields 4 to 6 servings.

Scituate was founded in 1667 and is the site of Rhode Island's largest reservoir. The name means "cold running water," or "Satuit" in an Indian dialect. The 92.8 square miles of watershed, built before the Depression, provides Greater Providence with water that is nationally recognized for its purity and quality. The reservoir, rich in natural beauty, also serves as a nesting ground for thousands of Canadian geese each spring.

Wild Rice with Pecans

The fruity flavor of this dish is a great complement to pork.

- ~ 1 cup uncooked wild rice
- ~ 5 1/2 cups chicken broth or chicken stock
- ~ 1 cup chopped pecans
- ~ 1 cup golden raisins
- ~ Grated rind of 1 large orange
- ~ 1/3 cup fresh orange juice
- ~ 1/4 cup olive oil
- ~ Thinly sliced scallions
- ~ Chopped fresh mint to taste
- ~ 1 1/2 teaspoons salt

Rinse the wild rice under cold water. Bring to a boil with the chicken broth in a medium heavy saucepan. Reduce the heat and simmer for 30 to 45 minutes or just until the rice is tender. Drain in a colander lined with a thin towel. Combine with the pecans, raisins, orange rind, orange juice, olive oil, scallions, mint and salt in a bowl and mix gently. Adjust the seasonings. Let stand for 2 hours to develop the flavors. Serve at room temperature. Yields 6 servings.

Fettuccini Alfredo with Pesto

This dish may be prepared with spinach fettuccini or any flat pasta. Serve it with Saintsbury Pinot Noir, 1993, or St. Francis Chardonnay, 1993.

- ~ 12 ounces uncooked fettuccini
- ~ Olive oil
- ~ 1 tablespoon minced garlic
- ~ 1 tablespoon flour
- ~ 1/4 cup melted butter
- ~ 1 cup (or more) light cream
- ~ 1 cup whipping cream
- ~ 1 teaspoon pepper
- ~ 1/2 to 3/4 cup grated Parmesan cheese
- ~ 1/4 cup pesto

Cook the pasta al dente. Rinse with cold water and drain. Toss with a small amount of olive oil in a bowl. Stir the garlic and flour into the melted butter in a large skillet over medium heat. Cook until bubbly, stirring constantly. Stir in the light and heavy cream and pepper. Cook until thickened, stirring constantly. Add the cheese and simmer for several minutes. Add the pesto and adjust the seasonings. Fold in the pasta. Simmer for 3 to 5 minutes or until heated through, stirring constantly. Yields 4 servings.

Fettuccini with Prosciutto and Portobello Mushroom in Roasted Garlic Cream Sauce

Serve this delightful dish with a salad of baby greens, focaccia bread and a Sakonnet America's Cup White wine. The sauce is similar to the one in Veal Medallions in a Basil Crust with Roasted Garlic Cream Sauce (page 100).

~ 1 portobello mushroom
~ 1 roasted red bell pepper, sliced into 2-inch strips

~ 6 slices prosciutto, cut into strips
~ 6 tablespoons pine nuts

~ Roasted Garlic Cream Sauce (below)
~ 16 ounces fettuccini
~ Salt to taste

Slice the mushroom and cut the slices into halves. Sauté in a large nonstick skillet until tender. Add the roasted pepper, prosciutto, pine nuts and the Roasted Garlic Cream Sauce. Simmer for 3 to 5 minutes or until heated through. Cook the pasta in salted boiling water in a saucepan for 6 to 7 minutes or until al dente; drain. Add the sauce and toss to mix well. Serve with Parmesan cheese. Yields 6 servings.

Roasted Garlic Cream Sauce

~ 1 tablespoon olive oil
~ 5 unpeeled cloves of garlic

~ 1/3 cup chopped shallots
~ 1 cup dry white wine
~ 6 tablespoons chopped pine nuts

~ 2 cups heavy cream
~ Salt and pepper to taste

Drizzle the olive oil onto a square of foil and place the garlic in the oil. Fold the foil to enclose the garlic and seal tightly. Roast at 350 degrees for 15 minutes or until tender. Peel the garlic and mash with a fork in a bowl. Sauté the shallots in a nonstick skillet over medium-high heat. Add the wine and pine nuts. Bring to a boil and boil until the liquid just covers the pine nuts. Stir in the cream. Cook until thickened, whisking constantly. Strain into a bowl and stir in the garlic purée, salt and pepper; keep warm. Yields 6 servings.

Complements

Federal Hill is a prominent Italian neighborhood in Providence known for its outstanding restaurants. The area was the site of the Providence Macaroni Riot in August of 1914. Food prices were rising internationally, and local businessman Frank Ventrone followed the trend by increasing the price of the pasta his business made for most Federal Hill residents. Angered that Ventrone would raise the price on their staple food, thereby further

Cavatelli with Sausage and Broccoli

Gnocchi is similar in size and texture to cavatelli and can also be used in this recipe. Try it with a Chateau St. Jean Fumé Blanc, 1992, or a Chateau St. Louis (Corbiere), 1993.

~ 1 (30-ounce) package frozen cavatelli

~ 1 (10-ounce) package frozen chopped broccoli

~ 6 thick links hot Italian sausage

~ 3/4 cup olive oil (about)

~ 3/4 cup grated Parmesan cheese (about)

Cook the cavatelli al dente and cook the broccoli until tender. Cook the sausage in a skillet. Remove from the casing and crumble. Combine the cavatelli, broccoli and sausage in a large bowl. Add the olive oil and cheese and mix lightly. Yields 6 servings.

burdening the
Italian community,
the community
rioted. After
breaking windows
on a block of
property Ventrone
owned, the rioters
marched into his
pasta business and
dumpted his stock
of macaroni into
the street. The next
day Ventrone
agreed that he had
overstepped the
bounds of ethnic
loyalty and lowered
his prices.

White Lasagna

Add one pound of sausage for a heartier dish. Serve with Castelgreve Chianti Classico, 1993, or Chiarlo Gavi, 1992.

- ~ 16 ounces lasagna noodles
- ~ 1/2 cup butter
- ~ 1/2 cup flour
- ~ Salt and pepper to taste
- ~ 4 cups milk
- ~ 4 eggs
- ~ 2 pounds ricotta cheese or low-fat ricotta cheese
- ~ 8 ounces grated Romano cheese
- ~ 1 pound mozzarella cheese or low-fat mozzarella cheese, sliced or shredded

Cook the noodles al dente; drain. Melt the butter in a saucepan and stir in the flour gradually. Cook over low heat until bubbly. Season with salt and pepper. Stir in the milk gradually. Cook until thickened, stirring constantly. Spread a small amount of the sauce in a lightly oiled 9x13-inch baking dish. Mix the eggs and the ricotta cheese in a bowl. Stir in the grated Romano cheese, salt and pepper. Layer the noodles, ricotta cheese mixture, mozzarella cheese and sauce in the prepared dish until all the ingredients are used. Bake at 350 degrees for 30 to 45 minutes or until bubbly. Yields 6 to 8 servings.

Pasta with Anchovies and Pignoli

This can be served either as a side dish or an entrée. Serve with Sakonnet Vidal Blanc or Newport Series Chardonnay.

- ~ 1 can anchovy fillets
- ~ 3/4 cup olive oil
- ~ 1/2 cup pignoli or coursely chopped walnuts
- ~ 1 large or 2 medium cloves of garlic, minced
- ~ 1 cup dry white wine
- ~ 16 ounces angel hair pasta, cooked
- ~ Freshly grated Parmesan cheese
- ~ Chopped Italian parsley

Drain the oil from the anchovies and combine the oil with the olive oil in a sauté pan. Break up the anchovies with a fork and add to the sauté pan. Add the pine nuts. Sauté for 5 minutes or until the pine nuts are golden brown. Add the garlic and wine. Cook over medium heat for 2 to 3 minutes. Combine with the pasta, cheese and parsley in a bowl and toss to mix well. Yields 4 to 6 servings.

Pasta Primavera

The heavy sauce is missing from this tasty version of the colorful favorite, making it lighter in calories, fats and cholesterol. Serve it with America's Cup White wine.

- ~ 2 cloves of garlic, crushed
- ~ 3 tablespoons butter
- ~ 1 tablespoon vegetable oil
- ~ 2 cups broccoli florets

- ~ 2 carrots, peeled, julienned
- ~ 2 zucchini, thinly sliced
- ~ 1 red bell pepper, cut into 3/4-inch pieces
- ~ 4 scallions, sliced

- ~ 16 ounces rotelli, cooked
- ~ Salt and pepper to taste
- ~ Grated Parmesan cheese

Sauté the garlic in the heated butter and oil in a large saucepan for 2 to 3 minutes or until golden brown. Add the broccoli, carrots, zucchini, bell pepper and scallions. Sauté over high heat until crisp-tender. Combine with the pasta in a serving bowl and toss to mix well. Season with salt and pepper. Top servings with Parmesan cheese. Yields 4 servings.

Rasta Pasta Sauce

The chef at Rue de l'espoir Restaurant recommends tossing this sauce with your favorite pasta shape and serving it with grilled boneless chicken breasts. Add a Vidal Blanc-Sakonnet or a Chardonnay-Stonington.

- ~ 3 cups chicken stock
- ~ 2 cups orange juice
- ~ 1/2 cup sesame oil
- ~ 1/2 cup oyster sauce
- ~ 1/2 cup honey

- ~ 1 cup tamari
- ~ 1/2 cup sherry
- ~ 1/4 cup chili paste
- ~ 2 tablespoons chopped garlic

- ~ 1 tablespoon ginger
- ~ 1 1/2 cups cornstarch

Combine the chicken stock, orange juice, sesame oil, oyster sauce, honey, tamari, sherry, chili paste, garlic and ginger in a saucepan. Bring to a boil. Blend the cornstarch with enough water to make a paste in a cup. Stir into the saucepan. Cook until thickened, stirring constantly. Yields 10 cups.

Pasta with Vodka and Tomato Sauce

For a special meal, serve this gourmet dish with Warm Spinach and Basil Salad (page 61) and a Beneziger Merlot, 1993, or an Altensino Rosso del Altesino, 1991.

~ 3/4 cup finely chopped shallots

~ 1/4 teaspoon crushed red pepper

~ 2 tablespoons olive oil

~ 1/2 cup vodka

~ 3/4 cup whipping cream

~ 3/4 cup tomato sauce

~ 1/2 cup oil-pack sun-dried tomatoes, chopped

~ 4 ounces prosciutto, thinly sliced, chopped

~ 2 tablespoons chopped fresh parsley

~ 2 tablespoons chopped fresh basil

~ Salt and pepper to taste

~ 2/3 cup grated asiago cheese

~ 8 ounces rigatoni or other tubular pasta, cooked al dente

Sauté the shallots and crushed red pepper in the olive oil in a heavy skillet over medium heat for 5 minutes or until the shallots are tender. Stir in the vodka and ignite. Cook for 2 minutes or until the flames subside, shaking the skillet occasionally. Increase the heat to high and stir in the cream. Cook for 5 minutes or until the mixture begins to thicken. Add the tomato sauce. Cook for 3 minutes or until thickened to the desired consistency. Add the sun-dried tomatoes, prosciutto, parsley, basil, salt, pepper and half the cheese and mix well. Toss with the pasta in a serving bowl and sprinkle with the remaining cheese. Yields 2 to 4 servings.

Complements

Straw and Hay

The Raphael Bar·Risto adds artichokes and roasted red peppers to this classic dish. Serve it with Jadot Moulin-A-Vent Beaujolais, 1993, or Cambria Chardonnay, 1993.

~ 6 cloves of garlic, chopped
~ 1/4 cup olive oil
~ 1/2 onion, thinly sliced
~ 1 tablespoon capers
~ 8 green Sicilian olives
~ 8 brine-cured black olives
~ 4 baby artichokes, cooked, cut into quarters
~ Crushed red pepper to taste
~ 1/2 cup dry white wine
~ 1 cup chopped tomato
~ 1 cup roasted red peppers
~ 1/4 cup chopped Italian parsley
~ Extra-virgin olive oil to taste
~ Salt and pepper to taste
~ 4 ounces egg fettuccini, cooked al dente
~ 4 ounces wheat fettuccini, cooked al dente
~ 1/2 cup Sardinian ricotta cheese

Sauté the garlic in 1/4 cup olive oil in a heated sauté pan over medium-high heat until golden brown. Add the onion, capers, olives, artichokes and crushed red pepper. Sauté until the onion is tender. Add the wine, stirring to deglaze the sauté pan. Stir in the tomato and roasted peppers. Simmer for 2 minutes. Stir in the parsley, additional olive oil, salt and pepper. Add the pasta and toss to mix well. Spoon onto a serving platter and sprinkle with the cheese. Yields 2 servings.

Squash Ravioli with Sage Cream Sauce

You will enjoy the different flavor combination of the ingredients in this delicious recipe.

~ 1/4 cup pignoli or walnuts
~ 2 tablespoons clarified butter
~ 2 cups whipping cream
~ 1/2 teaspoon finely ground dried sage
~ 1 ounce frangelico or amaretto
~ Salt and pepper to taste
~ 12 fresh or frozen squash or pumpkin ravioli
~ 1/4 cup chopped parsley

Sauté the pignoli in the butter in a large heavy skillet over medium heat for one to two minutes or just until golden brown. Add the cream, sage and liqueur. Cook for 5 to 8 minutes or until thickened to the desired consistency. Season with salt and pepper. Cook the ravioli al dente in salted boiling water in a large saucepan; drain. Combine with the sauce in a serving bowl and toss lightly to mix. Sprinkle with the pignoli and parsley. Yields 2 servings.

Vermicelli alla Siracusana

You can prepare this easy dish in just minutes. Serve it with Marcarini Dolchetto d'Alba, 1991, or Ruffino Labaio, 1992.

~ 2 cloves of garlic, sliced
~ 1/4 cup olive oil
~ 1 1/2 pounds tomatoes, coarsely chopped, or 2 (28-ounce) cans plum tomatoes, chopped
~ 1/4 cup capers
~ 8 kalamata olives, chopped
~ 6 anchovies, finely chopped
~ 4 fresh basil leaves, chopped
~ 1/2 teaspoon salt
~ 16 ounces vermicelli or fedelini, cooked

Sauté the garlic in the heated olive oil in a saucepan until light brown. Add the tomatoes and bring to a simmer. Stir in the capers, olives and anchovies. Simmer, covered, for 5 to 10 minutes or to the desired consistency. Stir in the basil and salt. Toss with the pasta in a serving bowl. Yields 6 servings.

Spicy Peanut Noodles

This is a great dish to take along for summer picnics or sailing outings.

~ 1/4 teaspoon red
  pepper
~ 5 tablespoons
  peanut oil
~ 1/2 cup plus 2
  tablespoons chunky
  peanut butter
~ 3 to 4 tablespoons
  minced green onions

~ 3 tablespoons soy
  sauce or tamari
  sauce
~ 2 tablespoons malt
  vinegar
~ 1 to 2 teaspoons
  crushed garlic
~ 1 teaspoon sugar

~ 1/4 teaspoon
  crushed peppercorns
  or Szechuan
  peppercorns
~ 16 ounces Chinese
  egg noodles
~ 1 bunch spinach or
  watercress,
  parboiled, drained

Heat the red pepper in the peanut oil in a skillet. Combine with the
peanut butter, green onions, soy sauce, vinegar, garlic, sugar and
peppercorns in a bowl and mix well. Add water if a thinner consistency
is desired. Cook the noodles in water in a saucepan just until tender;
drain. Combine with the peanut sauce and spinach in a bowl and mix
gently. Serve at room temperature. Yields 8 to 10 servings.

Ricotta Gnocchi

Try this for a new twist on an old favorite. Serve it with Vodka and
Tomato Sauce (page 157). Serve it with America's Cup White wine.

~ 1 egg, beaten
~ 1 cup ricotta cheese

~ 1 tablespoon salt

~ 2 cups flour
~ Salt to taste

Blend the egg and ricotta cheese in a bowl. Mix one tablespoon salt with
the flour in a large bowl. Add the egg mixture and mix well, kneading
until the dough holds it shape. Shape into ropes 1/2 inch in diameter.
Cut into 3/4-inch pieces. Press and roll each piece, pressing lightly with
the back of a fork. Cook in salted boiling water in a saucepan until the
gnocchi rise to the surface. Serve with your favorite sauce.
Yields 2 to 4 servings.

A Tasteful

Reflection of

Historic

Rhode Island

Desserts

Desserts

Cakes

Candy and Cookies

Tarts and Pies

Desserts

Country Apple Crisp

Bake this in an attractive ovenproof dish and serve it directly from the dish. It is good hot or cold.

- ~ 4 cups sliced peeled baking apples
- ~ 2 tablespoons lemon juice
- ~ 1/2 cup flour
- ~ 1/2 cup packed brown sugar
- ~ 1 teaspoon cinnamon
- ~ 1/4 cup butter

Place the apples in a 9-inch baking dish. Sprinkle with the lemon juice. Mix the flour, brown sugar, cinnamon and butter in a bowl until crumbly. Sprinkle over the apples. Bake at 375 degrees for 30 minutes or until the apples are tender and the topping is golden brown. Yields 6 servings.

Apricot Mousse

Prepare this in advance and chill in the refrigerator for a refreshing finish to a company dinner.

- ~ 1 cup chopped dried apricots
- ~ 1/2 cup apricot preserves
- ~ 2 tablespoons amaretto
- ~ 1 cup whipping cream
- ~ 1/2 cup confectioners' sugar

Combine the apricots, preserves and amaretto in a bowl. Let stand for 30 minutes. Whip the cream in a bowl until soft peaks form. Fold in the confectioners' sugar and then the apricot mixture. Spoon into a serving bowl or 4 individual goblets. Chill until serving time. Yields 4 servings.

Chocolate Crepes with Ricotta Filling and Fresh Raspberry Coulis

This dessert takes a little more time, but the reviews will make it worth the trouble.

~ 3/4 cup flour
~ 3/4 cup milk
~ 3/4 cup water
~ 6 tablespoons nonalkalized baking cocoa

~ 3 large eggs
~ 1/4 cup sugar
~ 3 tablespoons melted unsalted butter

~ 1 teaspoon vanilla extract
~ 1/4 teaspoon salt
~ Ricotta Filling
~ Fresh Raspberry Coulis (page 165)

Combine the flour, milk, water, baking cocoa, eggs, sugar, butter, vanilla and salt in a food processor. Process for 15 to 25 seconds or until smooth, scraping the side once. Spoon into a medium bowl and cover with plastic wrap. Chill for one hour. Heat a 6-inch crepe pan over medium-high heat until a few drops of water skip on the surface. Grease the pan lightly. Add 3 tablespoons of the batter at a time, tilting the pan to coat evenly. Bake for one minute or until edges appear lacy and the bottom is light brown. Turn the crepe and bake for 15 to 30 seconds or until light brown on the other side. Remove crepes to waxed paper and repeat with the remaining batter, greasing the pan as needed. Spoon 1/4 cup of the Ricotta Filling onto each crepe. Fold each crepe over to enclose the filling and then over again to form a triangle. Place on a serving platter. Serve with the Fresh Raspberry Coulis. Yields 14 servings.

Ricotta Filling

~ 3/4 cup heavy cream
~ 2 tablespoons sugar
~ 1 tablespoon almond liqueur

~ 1 cup ricotta cheese or low-fat ricotta cheese

~ 2/3 cup miniature chocolate chips

Beat the cream and sugar in a medium mixing bowl at high speed until soft peaks form. Add the liqueur and ricotta cheese and beat at medium speed for 45 seconds or until thick. Fold in the chocolate chips. Chill, covered, until serving time. Yields 2 1/2 cups.

Chocolate Paté with Fresh Raspberry Coulis

The flavors of chocolate and fresh raspberries are an unbeatable combination in this elegant dessert from Judy Rush of the International Gourmet Society.

- ~ 1/2 cup heavy cream
- ~ 3 egg yolks, slightly beaten
- ~ 16 ounces semisweet chocolate, broken
- ~ 1/3 cup butter or margarine
- ~ 1/2 cup light corn syrup
- ~ 1 1/2 cups heavy cream
- ~ 1/4 cup confectioners' sugar
- ~ 1 teaspoon vanilla extract
- ~ Fresh Raspberry Coulis (below)

Line a 5x9-inch loaf pan with plastic wrap. Combine 1/2 cup cream with the eggs yolks in a small bowl and mix well. Melt the chocolate and butter with the corn syrup in a 3-quart saucepan over medium heat, stirring to mix well. Add the egg yolk mixture gradually. Cook for 3 minutes, stirring constantly. Cool to room temperature. Beat 1 1/2 cups cream with the confectioners' sugar and vanilla in a mixing bowl until soft peaks form. Fold evenly into the chocolate mixture. Spoon into the prepared pan. Chill for 8 hours or freeze for 3 hours. Invert onto a serving platter and remove the plastic wrap. Cut into 12 slices. Spoon the Fresh Raspberry Coulis onto the serving plates and top with the paté slices. Garnish with additional fresh raspberries. Yields 12 servings.

Fresh Raspberry Coulis

- ~ 1 1/2 cups fresh raspberries
- ~ 1/4 cup superfine sugar
- ~ 3 tablespoons lemon juice
- ~ 1 tablespoon raspberry liqueur

Process the raspberries in a blender until smooth. Strain through a fine sieve. Combine with the sugar, lemon juice and liqueur in a bowl and mix well. Add to the puréed raspberries. Chill until serving time.
Yields one cup.

Luscious Lemon Meringue Torte

This torte is especially beautiful with fresh raspberries and blueberries, but when they are out of season other fruits can be used. Serve it with Fresh Raspberry Coulis (page 165).

~ 4 egg whites
~ 1 cup sugar
~ 1/2 teaspoon vanilla extract
~ 4 egg yolks
~ 1/2 cup sugar
~ 3 tablespoons fresh lemon juice

~ 2 teaspoons grated lemon rind
~ 2 cups whipping cream
~ 1/4 cup sugar
~ 2 teaspoons vanilla extract

~ Fresh Raspberry Coulis (page 165)
~ Fresh raspberries, blueberries and thinly sliced lemons

Draw three 9-inch circles on baking parchment. Beat the egg whites in a mixing bowl until soft peaks form. Add one cup sugar very gradually, beating constantly until stiff peaks form. Fold in 1/2 teaspoon vanilla. Spread the meringue in circles on the baking parchment. Bake at 250 degrees for one hour. Let stand until firm and remove to a wire rack to cool completely. Beat the egg yolks with 1/2 cup sugar in a double boiler. Add the lemon juice and lemon rind. Cook over simmering water until the mixture thickens enough to coat the back of a spoon, stirring constantly. Cool to room temperature. Whip the cream in a mixing bowl until soft peaks form. Fold in 1/4 cup sugar, 2 teaspoons vanilla and cooled lemon sauce. Layer the meringues and filling in a 9-inch springform pan, ending with the lemon filling. Freeze until firm. Serve with Fresh Raspberry Coulis. Garnish with fresh raspberries and blueberries and thinly sliced lemons. Yields 6 servings.

Bourbon Peach Sauce

Bring a touch of southern cheer to your dessert table with this combination of peaches, bourbon and pecans. Packed in decorative jars, it makes a welcome holiday gift.

~ 3 large peaches, peeled, thinly sliced
~ 1 tablespoon lemon juice
~ 6 tablespoons unsalted butter
~ 1/2 cup packed brown sugar
~ 3 tablespoons whipping cream
~ 1/2 cup toasted pecan pieces
~ 1 tablespoon bourbon

Toss the peaches with the lemon juice in a bowl. Melt the butter in a saucepan over medium heat and stir in the brown sugar. Cook until bubbly and thickened. Add the cream one tablespoon at a time, stirring constantly. Cook for 3 minutes or until thickened and smooth. Stir in the peaches, pecans and bourbon. Cook for one minute longer, stirring constantly. Serve over vanilla ice cream. Yields 4 servings.

Peach Crisp

This recipe is from a contributor's grandmother. It is just as good with apples.

~ 5 to 6 cups sliced peaches
~ 1 cup flour
~ 1 cup sugar
~ 1 teaspoon baking powder
~ 3/4 teaspoon salt
~ 1 egg
~ 1/3 cup melted butter or margarine
~ Cinnamon to taste
~ 1 cup whipping cream, whipped or ice cream

Place the peaches in a greased 2 1/2-quart baking dish. Mix the flour, sugar, baking powder and salt in a bowl. Add the egg and mix with a fork until crumbly. Sprinkle over the peaches. Drizzle with the butter and sprinkle with the cinnamon. Bake at 350 degrees for 30 to 40 minutes or until golden brown. Serve warm with whipped cream or ice cream. Yields 8 servings.

The Governor Henry Lippitt House, built in 1865, is considered to be one of the most complete, authentic and intact Victorian houses in the country.

Poached Pears with Crème Anglaise

The poached pears would also be delicious served with Fresh Raspberry Coulis (page 165).

- ~ 6 Anjou pears
- ~ 1/2 cup sugar
- ~ 1 cup water
- ~ 2 tablespoons sherry
- ~ 1 cup chocolate sauce, heated
- ~ Crème Anglaise
- ~ Shaved chocolate

Peel the pears and cut them into halves, discarding the cores. Bring the sugar and water to a boil in a saucepan. Boil for one minute, stirring constantly. Add the sherry and pears. Poach, covered, over medium-low heat for 10 to 15 minutes or just until tender, turning several times. Cool in the syrup and chill for one hour; drain. Spoon several tablespoons of the chocolate sauce into 6 dessert bowls. Add the pears. Top with the Crème Anglaise and a drizzle of additional chocolate sauce. Garnish with shaved chocolate. Yields 6 servings.

Crème Anglaise

- ~ 4 large egg yolks
- ~ 1 cup sifted confectioners' sugar
- ~ 1/8 teaspoon salt
- ~ 2 tablespoons sherry
- ~ 1 cup heavy cream, chilled, whipped

Beat the egg yolks with the confectioners' sugar and salt in a double boiler. Add the sherry. Cook over simmering water for 5 to 7 minutes or until thickened to custard consistency, stirring constantly. Let cool to room temperature. Fold in the whipped cream. Chill until serving time. Yields 6 servings.

Pumpkin Cheesecake with Bourbon Sour Cream Topping

This is a wonderful dessert for the autumn and the holidays.

- ~ Cheesecake Crust (below)
- ~ 1 1/2 cups solid-pack pumpkin
- ~ 3 large eggs
- ~ 1/2 cup packed light brown sugar
- ~ 1 1/2 teaspoons cinnamon
- ~ 1/2 teaspoon ground ginger
- ~ 1/2 teaspoon grated nutmeg
- ~ 24 ounces cream cheese, softened
- ~ 1/2 cup sugar
- ~ 2 tablespoons heavy cream
- ~ 1 tablespoon cornstarch
- ~ 1 tablespoon bourbon (optional)
- ~ 1 teaspoon vanilla extract
- ~ 2 cups sour cream
- ~ 2 tablespoons sugar
- ~ 1 tablespoon bourbon (optional)
- ~ 16 pecan halves

Prepare the cheesecake crust (below). Combine the pumpkin, eggs, brown sugar, cinnamon, ginger and nutmeg in a bowl and whisk until smooth. Beat the cream cheese and 1/2 cup sugar in a mixing bowl until light. Add the cream, cornstarch, bourbon, vanilla and the pumpkin mixture and mix well. Spoon into the Cheesecake Crust. Bake at 350 degrees on the center oven rack for 50 to 55 minutes or until the center is set. Cool in the pan on a rack for 5 minutes. Combine the sour cream, 2 tablespoons sugar and one tablespoon bourbon in a bowl and whisk until smooth. Spread on the cheesecake. Bake for 5 minutes longer. Cool in the pan on a wire rack. Chill, covered, for 8 hours or longer. Place on a serving plate and remove the side of the pan. Top with the pecan halves. Yields 16 servings.

Cheesecake Crust

- ~ 3/4 cup graham cracker crumbs
- ~ 1/2 cup finely chopped pecans
- ~ 1/4 cup sugar
- ~ 1/4 cup packed brown sugar
- ~ 1/4 cup melted unsalted butter, cooled

Mix the cracker crumbs, pecans, sugar and brown sugar in a bowl. Add the butter and mix well. Press over the bottom and 1/2 inch up the side of a buttered 9-inch springform pan. Chill for one hour. Yields 16 servings.

Spiced Pumpkin Pudding with Walnut Cream

Try this with your next holiday dinner, a pleasant change for those pumpkin pie lovers in your family.

- ~ 3 cups half-and-half
- ~ 6 large eggs
- ~ 1/2 cup sugar
- ~ 1/2 cup packed brown sugar
- ~ 6 tablespoons unsulfured (light) molasses
- ~ 1 1/2 teaspoons cinnamon
- ~ 1 1/2 teaspoons ginger
- ~ 3/4 teaspoon nutmeg
- ~ 1/8 teaspoon (or more) ground cloves
- ~ 1/4 teaspoon salt
- ~ 1 1/2 (16-ounce) cans solid-pack pumpkin
- ~ Walnut Cream (below)

Bring the half-and-half to a simmer in a small saucepan. Beat the eggs, sugar, brown sugar, molasses, cinnamon, ginger, nutmeg, cloves and salt in a large bowl until smooth. Stir in the pumpkin and warm half-and-half. Spoon into a buttered shallow 8-cup baking dish. Place in a larger pan and add hot water halfway up the sides. Bake at 325 degrees for 50 minutes or until a knife inserted 2 inches from the center comes out clean. Cool completely. Serve chilled or at room temperature with Walnut Cream. Yields 8 servings.

Walnut Cream

- ~ 1 1/2 cups whipping cream, chilled
- ~ 3 tablespoons confectioners' sugar
- ~ 1 1/2 tablespoons spiced rum
- ~ 3/4 cup walnuts or pecans, toasted, finely chopped

Whip the cream in a medium mixing bowl until soft peaks form. Add the confectioners' sugar and rum and beat until smooth. Fold in the walnuts. Yields 8 servings.

Bread Pudding

The delicate flavor of this old-fashioned favorite will remind you of your grandmother's kitchen.

- ~ 1/2 cup raisins
- ~ Flour
- ~ 4 eggs
- ~ 2 cups milk
- ~ 1/2 cup sugar
- ~ 1/2 teaspoon vanilla extract
- ~ 4 slices fresh bread, cubed
- ~ Butter

Plump the raisins in warm water; drain and pat dry. Coat with a small amount of flour. Combine the eggs, milk, sugar and vanilla in a bowl and mix well. Stir in the bread cubes and raisins. Spoon into a greased baking dish. Dot with butter. Bake at 350 degrees for 30 minutes or until golden brown. Serve with whipped cream. Yields 6 servings.

Strawberry and Almond Dacquoise

This refreshing alternative to strawberry shortcake is from David Gaudet at La France Restaurant.

- ~ 1 1/2 cups sugar
- ~ 2 1/2 cups ground almonds
- ~ 8 egg whites
- ~ 1/2 teaspoon cream of tartar
- ~ Salt to taste
- ~ 1 quart strawberries
- ~ 1 pint (or more) whipping cream, whipped

Line 2 large sheet pans with baking parchment. Draw two 10-inch circles on the parchment and spread lightly with oil. Mix the sugar and almonds in a bowl and set aside. Beat the egg whites with the cream of tartar and salt in a mixing bowl until very stiff peaks form. Fold in the sugar and almonds. Spread into circles. Bake at 275 to 300 degrees for 40 minutes or until the meringues are crusty on top. Cool completely on the parchment. Remove carefully from the parchment. Reserve some of the strawberries for garnish and slice the remaining berries. Fold the strawberries into the whipped cream. Spread between the meringue layers and over the top and side of the dessert. Garnish with the reserved strawberries. Yields 10 to 12 servings.

Union Village in North Smithfield was the site of patriot Peleg Arnold's tavern. This tavern, built by Arnold's father in 1739, was licensed to serve the weary traveler passing along the Great Road to Worcester. Upon hearing of the battles of Lexington and Concord, Peleg took up the rebel cause and made his tavern a center for Revolutionary arms storage, recruitment and training. Not surprisingly, military training was good for

Presidential Carrot Cake

This moist cake can also be made in two nine-inch layers or a bundt pan.

- ~ 2 cups sugar
- ~ 1 1/2 cups vegetable oil
- ~ 3 eggs
- ~ 2 teaspoons vanilla extract
- ~ 2 1/4 cups flour
- ~ 2 teaspoons baking soda
- ~ 2 teaspoons cinnamon
- ~ 1/2 teaspoon nutmeg
- ~ 1 teaspoon salt
- ~ 2 cups shredded carrots
- ~ 2 cups flaked coconut
- ~ 1 (8-ounce) can crushed pineapple, drained
- ~ 1 cup chopped walnuts (optional)
- ~ Cream Cheese Frosting (below)

Combine the sugar, oil, eggs and vanilla in a large bowl and mix with a wooden spoon. Stir in the flour, baking soda, cinnamon, nutmeg and salt. Add the carrots, coconut, pineapple and walnuts and mix well. Spoon into a greased 9x13-inch cake pan. Bake at 350 degrees for 45 to 50 minutes or until a tester inserted in the center comes out clean. Cool in the pan for 5 minutes. Invert onto a wire rack to cool. Spread the Cream Cheese Frosting over the top and sides of the cooled cake. Yields 15 servings.

Cream Cheese Frosting

- ~ 6 ounces cream cheese, softened
- ~ 1/2 cup butter, softened
- ~ 1/4 cup milk
- ~ 2 teaspoons vanilla extract
- ~ 1/4 teaspoon salt
- ~ 3 to 4 cups confectioners' sugar

Combine the cream cheese, butter, milk, vanilla and salt in a mixing bowl and mix well. Add enough confectioners' sugar to make a spreading consistency, mixing until smooth. Yields 15 servings.

business and on drill days, thirsty minutemen could enjoy a tankard of punch, cider, grog, beer or a rum toddy while discussing rebellion and eating platters of cold meats, bread and cheese.

Buttermilk Chocolate Layer Cake

This cake is the delight of any chocolate lover.

~ 2 cups unbleached flour
~ 2 teaspoons baking powder
~ 1 1/2 teaspoons baking soda
~ 1/4 teaspoon nutmeg

~ 1/4 teaspoon salt
~ 1 cup unsalted butter, softened
~ 1 3/4 cups sugar
~ 4 ounces unsweetened chocolate, melted, cooled

~ 4 large eggs
~ 1 1/2 cups buttermilk
~ 1 teaspoon vanilla extract
~ Chocolate Frosting (below)

Sift the flour, baking powder, baking soda, nutmeg and salt together. Cream the butter and sugar in a mixing bowl until light and fluffy. Add the chocolate and mix well. Beat in the eggs one at a time. Blend the buttermilk and vanilla in a small bowl. Add to the chocolate mixture alternately with the flour mixture, beginning and ending with the flour mixture and mixing well after each addition. Spoon into 2 greased and floured 9-inch cake pans. Bake at 350 degrees for 30 to 35 minutes or until a tester comes out clean. Cool in the pans for several minutes. Remove the cake to a wire rack to cool completely. Spread Chocolate Frosting between the layers and over the top and side of the cake. Yields 16 servings.

Chocolate Frosting

~ 1 cup unsalted butter, softened
~ 8 ounces whipped cream cheese

~ 1 (16-ounce) package confectioners' sugar
~ 1 teaspoon vanilla extract

~ 5 ounces unsweetened chocolate, melted, cooled

Cream the butter and cream cheese in a mixing bowl until light. Add the confectioners' sugar and beat until fluffy. Beat in the vanilla and chocolate. Yields 16 servings.

Central Falls is the smallest city in Rhode Island. Acquired as part of Providence by Roger Williams in 1636, it is located near a falls on the Black-stone River. Charles Keene had the river dammed in 1780 and put a small mill on the site. While part of his mill was used to make tools, Keene also manu-factured chocolate. This industry, which lasted until the War of 1812, gave the small settlement the early names of Chocolateville and Chocolate Mills.

Chocolate Decadence Cake

This special treat is actually a flourless chocolate cake from the La France Restaurant.

~ 2 1/2 cups unsalted butter
~ 1 cup strong coffee or espresso
~ 18 ounces chocolate
~ 2 1/4 cups sugar

~ 9 large eggs, whisked
~ 1/2 cup raspberry jam
~ 2 tablespoons brandy or Cognac

~ Fresh or frozen raspberries
~ 1/4 cup whipped cream

Line a 10-inch springform pan with foil and butter the foil. Combine the butter, coffee, chocolate and sugar in a double boiler. Heat to 130 degrees, stirring to dissolve the sugar and mix well; do not overheat. Remove from the heat. Whisk a small amount of the hot mixture into the beaten eggs; whisk the eggs into the hot mixture. Spoon into the prepared pan. Bake at 250 degrees for 2 hours or until the center is set. Cool in the pan on a wire rack. Chill for 8 hours or longer. Place on a serving plate and remove the side of the pan. Combine the raspberry jam with the brandy in a small saucepan. Cook over low heat until the jam melts, stirring to mix well. Mix in the raspberries gently. Spoon the raspberry sauce onto the serving plates. Place slices of the cake in the sauce. Garnish with rosettes of whipped cream. Yields 16 servings.

Melting Chocolate Cakes

Master Chef George Karousos of the Sea Fare Inn shares this delectable recipe for individual chocolate cakes. Serve them with a berry coulis or vanilla sauce.

~ 2 cups unsalted butter

~ 16 ounces semisweet chocolate
~ 8 egg yolks

~ 10 eggs
~ 2 cups sugar
~ 2 cups flour

Melt the butter and chocolate in a double boiler. Combine the egg yolks, eggs and sugar in a mixing bowl and beat until the volume is tripled. Add the chocolate mixture and mix well. Whisk in the flour until smooth. Spoon into 16 greased and floured individual cake molds. Bake at 450 degrees for 8 to 10 minutes or until the cakes test done. Invert onto a wire rack to cool. Yields 16 servings.

Christmas Cranberry Cake

This colorful cake is fabulous for a Christmas celebration and would be even more beautiful baked in an attractive mold. The sweetness of the vanilla sauce is a perfect foil for the tartness of the cranberries.

~ 3 tablespoons butter, softened
~ 1 cup sugar
~ 2 cups flour

~ 1 tablespoon baking powder
~ 1/4 teaspoon salt
~ 1 cup milk

~ 3 cups cranberries
~ Vanilla Sauce (below)

Cream the butter and sugar in a mixing bowl until light and fluffy. Add the flour, baking powder, salt and milk and mix until smooth. Fold in the cranberries. Spread in a greased and floured 8- or 9-inch square cake pan. Bake at 350 degrees for 35 to 40 minutes or until the cake tests done. Cut into squares and serve immediately with the Vanilla Sauce.
Yields 9 servings.

Vanilla Sauce

~ 1 tablespoon flour
~ 1 cup sugar
~ 1/2 cup butter

~ 1/2 cup cream
~ 1 tablespoon white vinegar

~ 1 teaspoon vanilla extract

Mix the flour and sugar in a small saucepan. Add the butter, cream and vinegar. Cook over medium-high heat until the butter melts and the mixture is bubbly, stirring to blend well. Stir in the vanilla. Serve warm.
Yields 9 servings.

Marble House in
Newport was the
location of a
conference for
female social and
political activists in
July of 1914. The
proceeds went to
the Women's
Suffrage Movement
staunchly supported
by Ava Belmont and
her daughter,
Consuelo, Duchess
of Marlborough.
During the
conference, a tea
was held on the
grounds near Mrs.
Belmont's newly
completed Chinese
Teahouse. The

Cream Cheese Pound Cake

This basic pound cake is delicious with Fresh Raspberry Coulis (page 165), fresh berries or seasonal fruits.

~ 1 1/2 cups butter, softened
~ 8 ounces cream cheese

~ 3 cups sugar
~ 3 cups cake flour, sifted

~ 6 large eggs, al room temperature

Cream the butter and cream cheese in a mixing bowl until light. Add the sugar and beat until fluffy. Add the flour alternately with the eggs, mixing well after each addition. Spoon into a greased and floured 10-inch tube pan. Bake at 300 degrees for 1 1/2 hours. Cool in the pan on a wire rack for 20 minutes. Then remove the cake to the wire rack to cool completely. Yields 12 to 14 servings.

Lemon Pound Cake

You can vary this recipe by adding a cup of nuts and substituting vanilla for the lemon flavoring.

~ 1 cup butter, softened
~ 1/2 cup shortening
~ 3 cups sugar
~ 5 eggs

~ 3 cups cake flour
~ 1/2 teaspoon baking powder

~ 1 cup milk
~ 1 teaspoon lemon extract

Cream the butter and shortening in a mixing bowl until light. Add the sugar, beating until fluffy. Beat in the eggs. Add the flour and baking powder alternately with the milk, mixing well after each addition. Beat in the lemon extract; batter will be thick. Spoon into a greased and floured tube pan. Bake at 350 degrees for 1 1/2 hours or until the cake tests done. Cover with foil during the last 30 minutes if you prefer a less crunchy top. Cool in the pan for 10 minutes. Remove the cake to a wire rack to cool completely. Yields 16 servings.

Lemon Roll

You can substitute your favorite filling for the lemon filling in this basic sponge cake roll.

~ 4 egg whites
~ 1/2 cup sugar
~ 4 egg yolks
~ 1/4 cup sugar

~ 1/2 teaspoon vanilla extract
~ 2/3 cup flour
~ 1 teaspoon baking powder

~ 1/4 teaspoon salt
~ Lemon Filling (below)
~ Confectioners' sugar

Beat the egg whites with 1/2 cup sugar in a mixing bowl until stiff peaks form. Beat the eggs yolks in a medium mixing bowl until thick and lemon-colored. Add 1/4 cup sugar and vanilla and mix well. Fold into the egg whites. Sift the flour, baking powder and salt together and fold gently into the egg white mixture. Spoon into a 10x15-inch baking pan lined with baking parchment and smooth with a spatula. Bake at 375 degrees for 10 to 12 minutes or until golden brown. Invert onto a towel and remove the baking parchment. Roll in the towel and let stand until cool. Unroll the cake and spoon the Lemon Filling down the center. Roll the cake to enclose the filling. Place seam side down on a serving plate and dust with confectioners' sugar. Chill until serving time. Slice to serve.
Yields 12 servings.

Lemon Filling

You may not need all of the filling for the Lemon Roll, but your family won't mind.

~ 1 package lemon pudding and pie filling mix
~ 1/2 cup sugar

~ 3 tablespoons lemon juice
~ 1 3/4 cups boiling water

~ 2 egg yolks, beaten
~ 1 cup sour cream

Combine the pudding mix, sugar, lemon juice and boiling water in a double boiler and mix well. Cook over hot water until smooth. Stir a small amount of the hot mixture into the egg yolks; stir the eggs yolks back into the hot mixture. Cook until thickened, stirring constantly. Cool to room temperature. Stir in the sour cream. Chill in the refrigerator.
Yields 4 cups.

Buckeyes

If you like peanut butter cups, these are for you. Package them in decorative containers for holiday giving.

- ~ 2 cups butter, softened
- ~ 32 ounces peanut butter
- ~ 2 teaspoons vanilla extract
- ~ 3 (16-ounce) packages confectioners' sugar
- ~ 12 ounces (or more) chocolate chips
- ~ 1/4 bar paraffin

Cream the butter, peanut butter and vanilla in a mixing bowl until light. Add the confectioners' sugar gradually, mixing constantly until smooth. Shape into bite-size balls. Chill for 8 hours or longer. Melt the chocolate chips with the paraffin in a double boiler, stirring to mix well. Dip the peanut butter balls into the chocolate mixture with a wooden pick, leaving an "eye" uncovered. Dip into ice water immediately to set. Place on waxed paper to dry. Layer in a freezer container and store in the freezer. Yields 200 buckeyes.

Almond Toffee Squares

This is an easy and tasty treat to keep on hand for snacks and drop-in guests. The recipe makes enough for a crowd.

- ~ 1 cup butter, softened
- ~ 1 cup packed brown sugar
- ~ 2 teaspoons vanilla extract
- ~ 1/4 teaspoon salt
- ~ 2 cups flour
- ~ 1/2 teaspoon baking soda
- ~ 1 1/4 cups semisweet chocolate chips
- ~ 3/4 cup chopped slivered almonds

Cream the butter, brown sugar, vanilla and salt in a mixing bowl until light and fluffy. Mix the flour and baking soda together. Add 1/2 cup at a time to the creamed mixture, mixing well after each addition. Spread in a greased 10x15-inch baking pan. Bake at 350 degrees for 20 minutes or until golden brown. Sprinkle with the chocolate chips. Let stand until the chocolate chips begin to melt and spread evenly with a spatula. Sprinkle immediately with the almonds, pressing lightly into the chocolate. Chill for 10 minutes or until the chocolate is firm. Cut into squares. Cool completely in the pan. Store in an airtight container at room temperature for up to one week or freeze until needed. Yields 50 squares.

Apple Saucers

These cookies, so rich with spice, raisins and apples, are almost as good without the glaze. Either way, they are an autumn celebration when the first tart and flavorful apples come to hand.

- ~ 1/2 cup shortening or 1/4 cup shortening and 1/4 cup butter
- ~ 1 1/4 cups packed brown sugar
- ~ 2 eggs
- ~ 1/4 teaspoon lemon extract (optional)
- ~ 1 1/2 cups flour
- ~ 1/2 teaspoon baking powder
- ~ 1/2 teaspoon baking soda
- ~ 1 teaspoon cinnamon
- ~ 1/4 teaspoon nutmeg
- ~ 1/8 teaspoon ground cloves
- ~ 3/4 teaspoon salt
- ~ 1 1/2 cups chopped peeled tart apples
- ~ 1 cup raisins or currants
- ~ 1 cup rolled oats
- ~ 1 cup coarsely chopped walnuts
- ~ 1/4 cup apple juice or orange juice
- ~ 1 tablespoon butter, softened
- ~ 1 1/2 cups sifted confectioners' sugar
- ~ 2 to 3 tablespoons apple juice or orange juice

Beat the shortening in a mixing bowl until light. Add the brown sugar, mixing until fluffy. Beat in the eggs one at a time. Add the lemon extract. Sift the flour, baking powder, baking soda, cinnamon, nutmeg, cloves and salt together. Add half the dry ingredients to the brown sugar mixture. Stir in the apples, raisins, oats and walnuts. Add the juice and the remaining dry ingredients and mix well. Shape by tablespoonfuls into balls. Arrange spaced well apart on lightly greased cookie sheets and flatten slightly. Bake at 350 degrees for 13 to 15 minutes or until the tops are firm to the touch and light brown. Cool on the cookie sheets on a wire rack for several minutes. Blend the butter with the confectioners' sugar and enough apple juice to make of a glaze consistency. Brush on the warm cookies and remove the cookies to the wire rack to cool completely. Store in airtight containers. May shape by 1/4 cupfuls for larger cookies. Yields 2 1/2 dozen.

Cream Cheese Brownies

The only way to improve on basic brownies is with the rich cream cheese marbleizing in this recipe.

- ~ 3 ounces cream cheese, softened
- ~ 2 tablespoons butter, softened
- ~ 1/4 cup sugar
- ~ 1 egg
- ~ 1 tablespoon flour
- ~ 1/2 teaspoon vanilla extract

- ~ 1 package German's sweet chocolate
- ~ 3 tablespoons butter
- ~ 2 eggs
- ~ 3/4 cup sugar
- ~ 1/2 cup flour
- ~ 1/2 teaspoon baking powder
- ~ 1/4 teaspoon salt

- ~ 1/4 teaspoon almond extract
- ~ 1/2 cup chopped pecans

Beat the cream cheese with 2 tablespoons butter in a mixing bowl until light. Add 1/4 cup sugar and beat until smooth. Beat in one egg, one tablespoon flour and the vanilla; set aside. Melt the chocolate with 3 tablespoons butter in a saucepan, stirring to blend well; cool. Beat 2 eggs in a mixing bowl until thick and lemon-colored. Add 3/4 cup sugar, 1/2 cup flour, baking powder, salt and almond extract and mix well. Stir in the chopped pecans and the cooled chocolate mixture. Reserve one cup of the batter. Spread the remaining batter in a greased 9x9-inch baking pan. Spread the cream cheese mixture evenly over the top. Drop the reserved batter over the cream cheese mixture and swirl with a knife to marbleize. Bake at 350 degrees for 35 to 40 minutes or until the brownies test done. Cool on a wire rack and cut into squares. Yields 20 brownies.

Chocolate Chip Crunchies

The innkeeper at the 1811 House in Manchester, Vermont, makes these treats for her guests. They are great with hot chocolate or a cold glass of milk after a day in the snow.

- ~ 3 1/2 cups flour
- ~ 1 tablespoon baking soda
- ~ 1 teaspoon salt
- ~ 1/2 cup butter, softened
- ~ 1/2 cup margarine, softened
- ~ 1 cup sugar
- ~ 1 cup packed brown sugar
- ~ 1 egg
- ~ 1 tablespoon milk
- ~ 2 teaspoons vanilla extract
- ~ 1 cup vegetable oil
- ~ 1 1/2 cups cornflakes
- ~ 1 1/2 cups rolled oats
- ~ 12 ounces chocolate chips

Mix the flour, baking soda and salt together. Cream the butter, margarine, sugar and brown sugar in a mixing bowl until light and fluffy. Beat in the egg, milk and vanilla. Add the flour mixture alternately with the oil, mixing well after each addition. Stir in the cornflakes, oats and chocolate chips. Drop by heaping teaspoonfuls 3 inches apart on an ungreased cookie sheet. Bake at 350 degrees for 12 minutes or until golden brown. Remove the cookies to a wire rack to cool. Do not use corn oil margarine in this cookie. Yields 7 dozen.

Chocolate Chip Meringue Mint Cookies

These cookies are low in fat. For variety, substitute chopped mint cookies and cream chocolate bars for the chocolate chips and peppermint extract.

- ~ 3 egg whites
- ~ 1/2 teaspoon cream of tartar
- ~ Salt to taste
- ~ 1 teaspoon vanilla extract
- ~ 1/4 teaspoon peppermint extract
- ~ 1 cup sugar
- ~ 1 cup semisweet chocolate chips

Combine the egg whites, cream of tartar, salt and flavorings in a mixing bowl and beat until soft peaks form. Add the sugar gradually, beating constantly until peaks are stiff and glossy. Fold in the chocolate chips gently. Drop by scant tablespoonfuls 1 1/2 inches apart onto parchment-lined cookie sheets. Bake at 275 degrees for 25 to 30 minutes or just until set. Let stand on the cookie sheets until cookies are firm enough to be removed with a spatula; cool on wire racks. Yields 5 dozen.

Joe Frogger cookies were supposedly created by a man called Uncle Joe who lived on a frog pond in Marblehead, Massachusetts. The fishermen and sailors from Barrington and other bay towns loved these cookies because they never got stale, even on long sea voyages. Joe claimed that the secret to their freshness was the mixture of rum and sea water in his recipe.

(South County Museum 126)

Joe Frogger Cookies

This is a modern version of the traditional hardy cookies carried by sailors on long sea voyages. They no longer contain sea water, as they originally did. Recipe from the East Greenwich Preservation Society 137.

~ 1/2 cup shortening
~ 1 cup sugar
~ 1 egg, beaten
~ 1 cup molasses
~ 1/4 cup dark rum
~ 4 cups flour
~ 1 teaspoon baking soda
~ 2 teaspoons ginger
~ 1/2 teaspoon allspice
~ 1/2 teaspoon cloves
~ 1/2 teaspoon nutmeg
~ 1 teaspoon salt

Cream the shortening and sugar in a mixing bowl until light and fluffy. Beat in the egg, molasses and rum. Add the dry ingredients and mix well. Chill for 8 hours or longer. Shape the dough into one-inch balls. Place on greased cookie sheets and flatten slightly. Bake at 350 degrees until light brown. Cool on the cookie sheets for several minutes; remove the cookies to a wire rack to cool completely. Yields 8 dozen.

Coconut Pyramids

Arrange these on trays for a beautiful addition to your buffet or tea table or pack them in decorative tins for holiday giving.

~ 4 cups sweetened coconut
~ 1/2 cup sugar
~ 3 egg whites
~ Salt to taste
~ 2 tablespoons melted unsalted butter
~ 1/2 teaspoon almond extract
~ 1/2 teaspoon vanilla extract
~ 4 ounces semisweet chocolate chips
~ 1/2 teaspoon shortening

Combine the coconut, sugar, egg whites and salt in a large bowl and mix well with hands. Add the butter and flavorings and mix well. Chill for one hour or longer. Shape by tablespoonfuls into firmly compacted balls with moistened hands. Place on work surface. Flatten sides with a spatula to form pyramids. Arrange one inch apart on parchment-lined cookie sheets. Bake at 350 degrees for 15 to 20 minutes or just until edges are golden brown. Cool on the cookie sheets on a wire rack. Melt the chocolate chips and shortening in a double boiler, stirring occasionally. Dip each pyramid upside down in the chocolate, covering only the top 1/2 inch of the point. Let stand until firm. Yields 2 dozen.

Gingersnaps

Enjoy this New England spiced cookie with an afternoon cup of tea.

- ~ 3/4 cup butter, softened
- ~ 1 cup sugar
- ~ 1/4 cup molasses
- ~ 1 egg

- ~ 2 cups flour
- ~ 2 teaspoons baking soda
- ~ 1 teaspoon cinnamon

- ~ 1 teaspoon ground cloves
- ~ 1 teaspoon ginger
- ~ 1/4 teaspoon salt
- ~ Sugar

Cream the butter and one cup sugar in a mixing bowl until light and fluffy. Beat in the molasses and egg. Sift in the flour, baking soda, cinnamon, cloves, ginger and salt and mix well. Shape into one-inch balls and roll in sugar. Place 2 inches apart on a cookie sheet. Bake at 375 degrees for 10 to 15 minutes or until evenly browned but still slightly soft. Cool on the cookie sheet for several minutes; remove the cookies to a wire rack to cool completely. Yields 3 1/2 dozen.

Orange Chocolate Chippers

For variety, try this change from the traditional chocolate chip cookie.

- ~ 1 cup shortening
- ~ 3 ounces cream cheese, softened
- ~ 1 cup sugar
- ~ 2 eggs

- ~ 2 tablespoons grated orange rind
- ~ 2 teaspoons vanilla extract
- ~ 2 cups flour

- ~ 1 teaspoon salt
- ~ 6 ounces chocolate chips

Cream the shortening, cream cheese and sugar in a mixing bowl until light and fluffy. Beat in the eggs, orange rind and vanilla. Sift in the flour and salt and mix well. Stir in the chocolate chips. Drop by rounded teaspoonfuls onto a greased cookie sheet. Bake at 350 degrees for 10 minutes or until very light brown. Cool on the cookie sheet for several minutes; remove the cookies to a wire rack to cool completely. Yields 3 dozen.

Desserts

West Greenwich,
settled in 1709, is a
rural town traversed
by the New London
Turnpike. One of the
many early 19th
century taverns that
dotted the pike was
the Tillinghast-
Hazard Place on
Molasses Hill Road.
In addition to
running a coach
stop, the proprietors
also reportedly ran
a molasses factory
on their property.
This was not an
uncommon activity
in Rhode Island,
where unfortunately,
making molasses
was often part of the

Pepparkakor

If these last long enough to get stale, they are delicious dipped in coffee—an old world style cookie.

~ 1 cup butter or
   margarine, softened
~ 1 1/2 cups sugar
~ 1/2 cup molasses
~ 1/2 cup sour cream

~ 1 egg
~ 5 cups sifted flour
~ 1 1/2 teaspoons
   baking soda

~ 1 1/2 teaspoons
   ginger
~ 1/2 teaspoon white
   pepper
~ Confectioners' sugar

Cream the butter in a mixing bowl. Beat in the sugar, molasses, sour cream and egg. Sift in the flour, baking soda, ginger and white pepper and mix well. Chill in the refrigerator. Shape into small balls and roll in the confectioners' sugar, coating well. Place on a greased or parchment-lined cookie sheet. Bake at 375 degrees for 10 to 12 minutes or until firm; cookies will crack. Remove the cookies to a wire rack to cool. Store in an airtight container. Sprinkle with additional confectioners' sugar if desired before serving. Yields 8 to 9 dozen.

Pignoli Cookies

You can make the almond paste for this recipe by processing 2 cups whole blanched almonds with 1/2 cup sugar and adding 1 egg white and 1/4 cup almond syrup. Store it in the refrigerator for up to one day.

~ 1/2 cup sugar
~ 1/2 cup
   confectioners' sugar

~ 1/8 teaspoon salt
~ 8 ounces almond
   paste

~ 2 egg whites, lightly
   beaten
~ Pignoli (pine nuts)

Sift the sugar, confectioners' sugar and salt together and set aside. Break up the almond paste in a bowl and add the egg whites; beat until smooth. Stir in the sugar mixture. Drop by rounded teaspoonfuls 2 inches apart on a parchment-lined cookie sheet (Note: Parchment is a must.). Sprinkle with the pignoli and press lightly into the surface. Bake at 300 degrees for 20 minutes or until light brown. Cool on the cookie sheet for several minutes and remove the cookies to a wire rack to cool completely. Yields 3 dozen.

notorious triangular
or slave trade.
Molasses was
generally distilled
into rum, and many
merchants were also
actively involved in
the third side of
this triangle—
trading the rum for
African slaves, who
then were traded
in the West Indies
for more sugar
or molasses.

Raspberry Walnut Thumbprint Cookies

You can substitute pecans for the walnuts or other jam for the raspberry in this easy recipe.

~ 1 1/2 cups butter, softened
~ 1 cup confectioners' sugar
~ 1 egg
~ 1/2 teaspoon cinnamon
~ 2 3/4 cups flour
~ 1 1/2 cups finely chopped walnuts
~ 2 cups raspberry jam
~ 1 tablespoon lemon juice
~ Confectioners' sugar

Combine the butter, one cup confectioners' sugar, egg and cinnamon in a mixing bowl and beat until smooth. Mix in the flour and walnuts gradually. Chill for one hour. Shape into small balls and place on a greased or parchment-lined cookie sheet. Make an indentation in each cookie with the thumb. Combine the jam and lemon juice in a bowl. Fill the indentation with jam mixture. Bake at 375 degrees for 10 to 12 minutes or until light brown. Cool on the cookie sheet for several minutes; remove the cookies to a wire rack to cool completely. Coat with confectioners' sugar if desired. Yields 3 to 4 dozen.

Ring Cookies

This is a pastry-like cookie without the usual folding procedures.

~ 1/2 cake or envelope yeast
~ 1 cup heavy cream
~ 1 cup butter, softened
~ 2 cups flour
~ Sugar

Dissolve the yeast in the cream in a bowl. Chill overnight. Combine the butter and flour in a mixing bowl and mix until smooth. Add the cream mixture and mix to form dough, adding additional flour if needed. Roll to 1/8-inch thickness on a floured surface. Cut into small circles, then cut out an inner circle from each with a thimble. Dip into sugar, coating well on both sides. Place on a parchment-lined cookie sheet. Bake at 400 degrees for 10 to 20 minutes or until light brown. Cool on the cookie sheet for several minutes; remove the cookies to a wire rack to cool completely. Yields 5 dozen.

Rugelach

This elegant cookie will be at home on the finest tea table or dessert buffet, if the family doesn't find them first.

- ~ 1 cup unsalted butter, softened
- ~ 8 ounces cream cheese, softened
- ~ 1/4 teaspoon salt
- ~ 2 cups flour

- ~ 1/4 cup melted unsalted butter
- ~ 3/4 cup sugar
- ~ 2 teaspoons (or more) cinnamon

- ~ 1/2 cup finely chopped walnuts
- ~ 1 1/3 cups currants
- ~ 1 egg white
- ~ 2 tablespoons water

Beat one cup butter and cream cheese at high speed in a mixing bowl until light. Beat in the salt. Stir in the flour with a spoon. Shape into a log with floured hands and cut into 4 equal portions. Flatten each portion into a disc and wrap with plastic wrap. Chill for one hour or longer. Let one disk at a time stand at room temperature for 10 minutes. Roll out to 1/8-inch thickness between sheets of floured waxed paper. Remove the waxed paper. Brush with melted butter and sprinkle with a mixture of the sugar and cinnamon, reserving 1/4 cup cinnamon-sugar for the topping. Sprinkle with the walnuts and currants, pressing lightly into the surface. Cut each circle into 12 wedges. Roll from the wide ends to enclose the filling. Place point side down on a parchment-lined cookie sheet. Brush with a mixture of the egg white and water. Sprinkle with the reserved cinnamon-sugar. Bake at 375 degrees for 15 minutes or until golden brown. Cool on the cookie sheet for several minutes; remove the cookies to a wire rack to cool completely. Yields 4 dozen.

Desserts

Delectable Sugar Cookies

This is the perfect all-purpose cookie, beloved by all. It can be baked plain, filled as it is here, or cut into any shape and decorated or frosted to fit the occasion.

- ~ 3/4 cup shortening or softened butter
- ~ 1 cup sugar
- ~ 2 eggs
- ~ 1/2 teaspoon vanilla extract or lemon extract
- ~ 1 teaspoon baking powder
- ~ 2 1/2 cups flour
- ~ 1/2 to 1 teaspoon salt
- ~ 1 egg white, beaten
- ~ Jam

Cream the shortening and sugar in a mixing bowl until light and fluffy. Beat in the eggs and vanilla. Mix the baking powder, flour and salt together. Add to the creamed mixture and mix well. Dust the dough lightly with flour and wrap in plastic wrap; chill for one hour or longer. Roll on a floured surface and cut into circles or other desired shape. Brush half the circles with the egg white. Place a small dab of jam in the center of each and top with the remaining cookies, pressing the edges lightly to seal. Pierce the top with a fork and place on an ungreased cookie sheet. Bake at 350 degrees for 10 to 15 minutes or until the edges are light brown. Cool on the cookie sheet for several minutes; remove the cookies to a wire rack to cool completely. Yields 4 dozen.

Desserts

Smithfield, with over 100 acres of orchards, is considered apple country. Each year, thousands of tourists come to this scenic area to enjoy both the beauty of the spring apple blossoms and the bounty of the fall apple harvest. The town's orchard industry began in the 1880s, with the cultivation of over a dozen varieties of apples, peaches and berries. Today, the orchards are open to the public

Pastiche's Apple Tart

Pastiche Fine Desserts serves this at room temperature or warmed very slightly with a caramel crème anglaise, but it would also be good with vanilla ice cream or lightly sweetened whipped cream.

~ 1/2 cup sugar
~ 1 tablespoon cornstarch
~ 1/2 teaspoon cinnamon
~ 2 tablespoons unsalted butter

~ 4 large baking apples, peeled, grated or finely chopped
~ 2 tablespoons water
~ Pastiche's Tart Shell (below)

~ 3 to 4 large baking apples, peeled, sliced
~ 1/4 cup sugar
~ 1 teaspoon cinnamon
~ Apricot jam

Mix 1/2 cup sugar, cornstarch and 1/2 teaspoon cinnamon together. Melt the butter in a large saucepan. Add the grated apples, water and sugar mixture. Simmer until the apples are tender and the mixture is clear, stirring frequently. Cool to room temperature. Spoon into the tart shell. Arrange the apple slices in a decorative pattern over the filling. Sprinkle with a mixture of 1/4 cup sugar and one teaspoon cinnamon. Bake at 350 degrees for 45 minutes. Cool on a wire rack. Melt apricot jam with just enough water to thin to the desired consistency in a saucepan. Brush over the tart. Yields 8 to 10 servings.

Pastiche's Tart Shell

~ 1 1/2 cups flour
~ 2 tablespoons sugar
~ Salt to taste

~ 1/2 cup butter, chilled, chopped
~ 1 egg yolk

~ 1 tablespoon cold water

Sift the flour, sugar and salt into a large bowl. Cut in the butter until the mixture resembles coarse crumbs. Add the egg yolk and water and mix just until the mixture forms a dough. Shape into a ball and flatten slightly. Chill, wrapped in plastic wrap, for several hours. Roll into a 13-inch circle on a lightly floured surface. Fit into an 11-inch tart pan. Place in the freezer for one hour. Line the pastry with foil and pie weights. Bake at 350 degrees for 20 minutes or until golden brown.
Yields one tart shell.

each fall, allowing visitors to pick their own fruit. The orchard farm stands also sell fresh apple products such as cider, pies, jelly and apple butter.

Chocolate Mousse Tart

Make this in advance for any occasion, from an elegant dinner to a family reunion.

~ 3 cups chocolate wafer crumbs
~ 1/2 cup melted butter
~ 16 ounces semisweet chocolate
~ 2 eggs
~ 4 egg yolks

~ 2 cups whipping cream
~ 6 tablespoons confectioners' sugar
~ 4 egg whites, at room temperature

~ 4 ounces semisweet chocolate
~ 1 teaspoon shortening
~ 2 cups whipping cream
~ Sugar to taste

Mix the cookie crumbs and melted butter in a bowl. Press over the bottom and side of a 10-inch springform pan. Chill for 30 minutes. Melt 16 ounces chocolate in a double boiler and cool slightly. Add the eggs first and then the egg yolks to the chocolate, mixing well after each addition. Beat 2 cups whipping cream in a mixing bowl until it begins to thicken. Add the confectioners' sugar gradually, beating constantly until soft peaks form. Beat the egg whites in a mixing bowl until stiff but not dry. Fold a small amount of the whipped cream mixture and the egg whites into the chocolate mixture. Fold the rest of the mixtures evenly into the chocolate. Spoon into the tart shell. Chill for 6 hours. Melt 4 ounces chocolate with the shortening in a double boiler. Coat the underside of waxy 2-inch leaves with the chocolate and chill or freeze until firm. Peel the leaves carefully from the chocolate layer. Place the tart on a serving plate and remove the side of the pan. Beat 2 cups whipping cream with sugar to taste in a mixing bowl until soft peaks form. Spread 3/4 of the whipped cream over the tart. Pipe the remaining whipped cream into a rosette in the center and trim with a decorative edge. Arrange the chocolate leaves around the rosette. Yields 16 servings.

Paradise Avenue in Middletown was the address of Mrs. Clara Whitman's Pie House in the 1920s. Patrons were mostly boys from St. George's School, an exclusive preparatory school nearby. Among Mrs. Whitman's clients were John Jacob Astor and Prince Braganza. The boys were sometimes without money, so Mrs. Whitman kept a running account on which she eventually collected payment.
(Middletown Historical Society)

Jumbleberry Pie

Take advantage of the delicious berries of summer all jumbled together in this wonderful pie.

- ~ Pâte Brisée (below)
- ~ 1 1/2 cups sugar
- ~ 1/3 cup cornstarch
- ~ 1/8 teaspoon grated nutmeg
- ~ 1/8 teaspoon cinnamon

- ~ 3 cups blackberries
- ~ 3 cups raspberries
- ~ 3 cups blueberries
- ~ 1/4 cup fresh lemon juice

- ~ 1 tablespoon unsalted butter, chopped
- ~ 1/4 cup half-and-half
- ~ Sugar to taste

Roll half the pastry to 1/8-inch thickness on a lightly floured surface. Fit into a deep 9-inch pie plate; trim the edge, leaving a 1/2-inch overhang. Chill in the refrigerator. Mix 1 1/2 cups sugar, cornstarch, nutmeg and cinnamon in a bowl. Add the blackberries, raspberries, blueberries and lemon juice and toss lightly. Spoon into the pie shell, mounding in the center. Dot with the butter. Roll the remaining pastry into one 14-inch circle and place over the filling; trim the edge, leaving a one-inch overhang. Fold the top pastry over the bottom and press to seal. Brush with the half-and- half and cut vents. Sprinkle with additional sugar and place on a baking sheet. Bake at 425 degrees on the center oven rack for 20 minutes. Reduce the oven temperature to 375 degrees and bake for 35 to 40 minutes longer or until golden brown. Serve with ice cream. Yields 8 servings.

Pâte Brisée

- ~ 2 1/2 cups flour
- ~ 1 teaspoon sugar
- ~ 1 teaspoon salt

- ~ 1 cup unsalted butter, chilled, chopped

- ~ 1/4 to 1/2 cup ice water

Combine the flour, sugar, salt and butter in a food processor and process for 10 seconds or until the mixture resembles coarse crumbs. Add the ice water one drop at a time, processing constantly just until the mixture forms a dough; do not process longer than 30 seconds. Chill, wrapped in plastic wrap, for one hour. Yields 2 pastries.

Mocha Ice Cream Toffee Pie

This is so easy to do and is sure to please everyone.

~ Ladyfingers, split
~ 1/2 gallon chocolate ice cream, softened
~ 1 quart coffee ice cream, softened
~ 6 ounces brickle chips or crushed toffee bars
~ 3 tablespoons instant coffee
~ 1/4 cup Kahlúa

Line the bottom of a 10-inch springform pan with ladyfingers. Arrange the remaining ladyfingers vertically around the side. Combine the chocolate ice cream, coffee ice cream, brickle chips and coffee granules in a bowl and mix well. Stir in the liqueur. Spoon into the prepared pan and freeze until firm. Let stand at room temperature for 15 minutes before serving. Top with whipped cream and chocolate curls. Yields 10 to 12 servings.

Raspberry Crumb Pie

This is, of course, better with fresh raspberries, but if you freeze some raspberries in season, you can enjoy this treat all year round.

~ 1 cup sugar
~ 1/3 cup flour
~ 2 large eggs, lightly beaten
~ 1 1/3 cups sour cream
~ 1 teaspoon vanilla extract
~ 3 cups fresh or frozen raspberries
~ 1 unbaked 9-inch pie shell (see pastry recipe on page 68)
~ 1/3 cup flour
~ 1/3 cup packed brown sugar
~ 3 tablespoons butter, softened
~ 1/3 cup chopped pecans
~ Whipped cream
~ Fresh raspberries

Combine the sugar, 1/3 cup flour, eggs, sour cream and vanilla in a bowl and mix well. Fold in 3 cups raspberries. Spoon into the pie shell. Bake at 400 degrees for 30 to 35 minutes or until the center is set. Combine 1/3 cup flour, brown sugar, butter and pecans in a bowl and mix until crumbly. Sprinkle over the hot pie. Bake for 10 minutes longer or until the topping is golden brown. Garnish with whipped cream and additional raspberries. Yield 6 to 8 servings.

Strawberry Meringue Pie

Pick a dry day to make meringue; use egg whites at room temperature and a clean dry bowl for the best results.

~ 3 egg whites, at room temperature
~ 1 cup sugar
~ 1 teaspoon vanilla extract

~ 24 butter crackers
~ 1/2 cup pecans
~ 1/4 teaspoon baking powder
~ 1 cup heavy cream

~ 2 tablespoons sugar
~ 1 pint strawberries, sliced

Beat the egg whites in a mixing bowl until soft peaks form. Add one cup sugar and the vanilla gradually, beating constantly until stiff peaks form. Process the crackers with the pecans in a food processor until crumbly. Fold into the egg white mixture with the baking powder. Spread the egg white mixture into a 9-inch pie plate to form the pie shell. Bake at 350 degrees for 30 minutes. Cool to room temperature. Whip the heavy cream with 2 tablespoons sugar in a mixing bowl until soft peaks form. Fold in the strawberries. Spoon into the meringue shell. Chill for 3 hours. Yields 6 to 8 servings.

French Canadian Butter Tarts

Make a big batch of these and watch them disappear. On a busy day, increase the recipe by one-half and make 36 miniature tart shells with two all-ready pie pastries.

~ 1 egg, beaten
~ 1/3 cup melted butter
~ 1 cup packed light brown sugar

~ 2 tablespoons milk
~ 1 teaspoon vanilla extract
~ 1/2 cup raisins or nuts

~ 24 unbaked tart shells (see pastry recipe on page 68)

Combine the egg, butter, brown sugar, milk and vanilla in a bowl and mix well. Stir in the raisins. Spoon into the tart shells. Bake at 350 degrees for 15 minutes. Yields 24 tarts.

A Tasteful

Reflection of

Historic

Rhode Island

Shutters

Shutters

Index of Photographs

Photography Credits:

Christine Barton, Angell Photography/Ruth A.B. Clegg, John Forasté/ Brown University, Doug Gray, Visuals Photography, Inc./Doreen Iafrate, Beth Ludwig, Paul Roberti, Susannah Snowden

Works Cited

Burke, Helen N. **Foods from the Founding Fathers.** Newport, RI: Newport Press, 1978.

Conley, Patrick T. **An Album of Rhode Island History, 1636–1986.** Norfolk, VA: Donning Company Publishers, 1986.

East Greenwich Preservation Society. **A Legacy of Greenwich Recipes from Generation to Generation.** Providence, 1983.

Middletown Historical Society. Information from Archivist Mary Bellagamba. Middletown, RI, 1994.

Norton, Katzman; Escott, Chudacoff; and Paterson, Tuttle. **A People and a Nation: A History of the United States, Volume II.** Boston, MA: Houghton Mifflin Company, 1990.

Pettaquamscutt Historical Society. Information from President Mark Archambeault and Bill Metz. South Kingstown, RI, 1995.

Preservation Society of Newport County. **The Chinese Teahouse, Marble House.** Newport, RI, 1980.

Simister, Florence P. **Streets of the City: An Anecdotal History of North Kingstown.** North Kingstown, RI, 1974.

South County Museum Association. **Country Kitchen Cookbook.** Narrangansett Press, Narragansett, RI, 1982.

Watson, Walter L. **History of the Town of Jamestown on Conanicut Island.** Providence, RI, 1949.

Bibliography

Amaral, Claudia. **Brown and Hopkins Country Store.** Providence, RI, 1992.

Arem, Joel E. **Color Encyclopedia of Gemstones.** New York, NY, 1977.

Bayles, Richard M., ed. **History of Newport County, Rhode Island.** New York, NY, 1988.

Block Island Historical Society, **Block Island Cookbook.** Providence, RI, 1962.

Burke, Helen N. **Foods from the Founding Fathers.** Newport, RI, 1978.

Clarke, Howard L., ed. **A History of the Town of Smithfield.** Providence, RI, 1976.

Conley, Patrick T. **An Album of Rhode Island History, 1636–1986.** The Donning Company, Norfolk, VA, 1986.

Conley, Patrick T. and Paul R. Campbell. **Providence: A Pictorial History.** The Donning Company, Norfolk, VA, 1982.

Conley, Patrick T., Robert Owen Jones and William McKenzie Woodward. **The State House of Rhode Island, An Architectural and Historical Legacy.** Rhode Island Historical Society and Rhode Island Historic Preservation Commission. Providence, RI, 1988.

D'Amato, Donald A. **Coventry Celebration: A Pictorial Celebration.** Virginia Beach, VA, 1991.

East Greenwich Preservation Society. **A Legacy of Greenwich Recipes from Generation to Generation.** Providence, RI, 1983.

Furnas, J.C. **The Americans—A Social History of the United States, 1587–1914.** New York, NY, 1969.

Glubok, Shirley, ed. **Home and Child Life in Colonial Days.** Toronto, Ontario, 1969.

Hale, Stuart O. **Narragansett Bay: A Friend's Perspective.** Narragansett, RI, 1980.

Haley, John W. **The Old Stone Bank History of Rhode Island, Volume II.** Providence, RI, 1931.

Hazard, Thomas R. **The Jonny Cake Letters.** Providence, RI, 1880.

Henshaw, John. **The Tale of the Clam; A Historical Reminiscence of Rhode Island.** Providence, RI, 1885.

Historical Society of Smithfield. **Historic Smith Appleby House circa 1696.** Smithfield, RI, 1994.

Kellner, George H., and Stanley J. Lemons. **Rhode Island The Independent State.** Woodland Hills, CA, 1982.

National Park Service, U.S. Department of the Interior. **The Blackstone River Valley.** Boston, MA, 1993.

Norton, Katzman, Escott, Chudacoff, Paterson, Tuttle. **A People and a Nation: A History of the United States, Volume II.** Boston, MA, 1990.

Peters, Russell. **Clambake—A Wampanoag Tradition.** Minneapolis, MN, 1992.

Pettaquamscutt Chapter Daughters of the American Revolution. **Facts and Fancies Concerning North Kingstown, Rhode Island.** Pawtucket, RI, 1989.

Preservation Society of Newport County. **The Chinese Teahouse—Marble House.** Newport, RI, 1980.

Providence Journal. "Accent." Providence, RI, 6/6/1974.

Providence Journal Bulletin. "City Life." Providence, RI, 2/4/1987.

Providence Sunday Journal. "Countylife." Providence, RI, 3/14/1948.

Rawson, Marion N. **When Antiques Were Young: A Story of Early American Social Customs.** New York, New York, 1931.

Rhode Island Historical Preservation Commission. **Historic and Architectural Resources of Bristol, Burrillville, Charlestown, Cumberland, Glocester, Lincoln, Middletown, North Smithfield, Portsmouth, Richmond, Smithfield, South Kingstown, Tiverton, West Greenwich and Westerly.**

Rhode Island Historical Preservation Commission. **Statewide Historical Preservation Report for Central Falls, Cranston, Cumberland, East Providence, Exeter, Foster, Hopkinton, Johnston and Woonsocket.**

Rhode Island Historical Society. **A Most Magnificent Mansion.** Providence, RI, 1985.

Rhode Island Historical Society and the Department of State Library Services. **What a Difference a Bay Makes.** Providence, RI, 1993.

Rhode Island Seafood Council. **Quahog Cookery—A Complete Guide.** Providence, RI, 1981.

Rhode Island Tourism Division. Department of Economic Development. **Rhode Island, America's First Resort.** Providence, RI, 1994.

Scituate Bicentennial Committee. **Scituate Receipts and Anecdotes.** Providence, RI, 1976.

Simister, Florence P. **Streets of the City: An Anecdotal History of North Kingstown.** North Kingstown, RI, 1974.

Society for the Propagation of the Jonnycake. **The Jonnycake Cookbook.** Providence, RI, 1986.

South County Museum. **Country Kitchen Cookbook.** Narragansett, RI, 1982.

Steinberg, Sheila, and Cathleen McGuigan. **Rhode Island An Historical Guide.** Providence, RI, 1976.

Stetson, Barbara S. **The Island Cookbook.** Boston, MA, 1980.

Watson, Walter L. **History of Jamestown on Conanicut Island.** Providence, RI, 1949.

Woodward, William McKenzie and Edward Sanderson. **Providence: A City-Wide Survey of Historic Resources.** Ed. David Chase, Foreword by Antoinette F. Downing. State-Wide Historical Preservation Report P-P-7, Rhode Island Preservation Commission, Providence, RI, 1986.

The Woonsocket Call. "Looking Back." Woonsocket, RI, 1/10/1988.

Index of Recipe Testers

Our gratitude goes out to the recipe testers and their families for giving not only their time but also financial support to ensure the highest quality possible. A special thank you goes to Sherrie Kimball for testing the most recipes.

Melissa Bauer	Beth Kinder
Sherry Brown	Kathleen Lee
Lisa Bruzzese	Melissa Lolli
Ruth Clegg	Virginia Mead
Elaine Colarusso	Mindy Morley
Valerie Conner	Donna Nicholson
Kim Curtis	Heather Paolino
Debra Cusack	Susan Petrocelli
Constance Danforth	Christine Phelps
Judith DePatie	Alicia Reynolds
Cindy Donadio	Dawn Roch
Nancy Dorsey	Monica Rogers
Amy Dressler	Elizabeth Smith
Lori Elias	Patricia Smolley
Karen Flynn	Karen Tarantino
Mary Gibbs	Angela Thomas
Holly Grace	Kathy Tipirneni
Kay Holley	Janet Wagner
Mary Jacobs	Penelope Wartels
Leslie Kellogg	Lisa Wright
Carolyn Killian	Jan Xillas
Sherrie Kimball	Carol Yarnell

Index of Contributors

The Windows Committee and the Junior League of Rhode Island, Inc., expresses grateful appreciation to League members, restaurants, family and friends who contributed their favorite recipes to **Windows, A Tasteful Reflection of Historic Rhode Island**. A special thank you goes to Sherrie Kimball for submitting the most recipes. We deeply regret that we were unable to include all of the wonderful recipes that were submitted, due to availability of space. We hope we have not inadvertently excluded anyone from this list.

Dominic Agostini
Donna Bachini
Linda Bainer
Christine Barton
Claire Bauer
Melissa Bauer
Mary Bellagamba
Martha Beveridge
Mary Beveridge
V. Black
Sharleen Bowen
Shirley Bradley
Trish Brakenhoff
Barbara Breiding
Ernest Brown
Sherry Brown
Donna Buchrer
Lisa Bruzzese
Reina Burman
Lois Campbell
Louise Carlin
Ruth Clegg
Anne Cline
Elaine Colarusso
Lucy Colarusso
Peggy Colette
Susan Collier
Millie Colwell
Valerie Conner
Christine Craun
Marguerite Crocker
Lynn Culp
Kim Curtis
Debra Cusack
Joanne DeCristofaro

Anna DeLuca
Marie DeLuca
Judith DePatie
Nancy Dorsey
Amy Dressler
Lori Elias
Susan Esposito
Robert Ferreira
Karen Flynn
Sheila Fontaine
Phyllis Fragola
Lathie Gannon
Leslie Gardner
Barbara Gaspar
Mary Gibbs
Ann Glosson
Sue Goldman
Holly Grace
Cherie Greene
Pam Greene
Mildred Hanson
Ann Harvey
Susan Hawkins
Penelope Hess
Kay Holley
Penny Hommeyer
Martha Hough
Nancy Hurd
Martha Jacobs
Mary Jacobs
Virginia Johnson
Leslie Kellogg
Carolyn Killian
Catherine Killian
Sherrie Kimball

Beth Kinder
Kelly Kologne
Barbara Lamy
Barbara Lardner
Kathleen Lee
Wendy Leicht
Darlene Lepore
Martha Lindstrom
Susan Lipscomb
Melissa Lolli
Cynthia Macliver
Lyn Mangiapane
Linda Martin
Amy Mastrangelo
Dorothy McCulloch
Kristen McCullough
Fran McKendall
Patricia McStay
Carl Mead
Marybeth Mead
Virginia Mead
John Mendillo
Margaret Menzies
Lucia Mezzancello
Melanie Mezzancello
Rob Migliaccio
Leslie Mitchell
Sandy Moberly
Mindy Morley
Mrs. Henry Moss
Margaret Narcizo
Mimi Nash
Shirley Neto
Donna Nicholson
Mary O'Brien

Ellie O'Neill
Joanne Orabone
Ann Orsini
Jill Palla
Myra Palla
Donna Paolino
Ethel Paolino
Heather Paolino
Susan Petrocelli
Cheryl Petterutti
Christine Phelps
Joan Prendergast
Karen Rakitt
Meg Rankin
Alicia Reynolds
Christine Rhodes
Dawn Roch
Christine Rogers
Rosa Rossi
Jill Sabatine
Tina Saker
Yoslaida Santos

Sylvia Sapir
Charles Savore
Nancy Scarton
Jane Schwab
Cheryl Serra
Dorothy Shaw
Lucy Simeone
Susan Skowran
Elizabeth Smith
Shirley Smith
Patricia Smolley
Virginia Smolley
Patricia Stell
David Stewart
Paula Surrette
Lolly Swain
Catherine Thenault
Angela Thomas
Ann Thorndike
Kathy Tipirneni
Jo Anne Urion
Julie Vallante

Julie Vanier
Dot Voccio
Janet Wagner
Dorothy Walker
Rosemary Weddle
Mary Whitaker
Michelle White
Tamara Wilson
Wayne Wilson
Eamma Sue Wing
Rita Wood
Emmett Wright
Lisa Wright
Jan Xillas
Michael Yeamans
Ann Marie Yankun
Carol Yarnell
Robert Yarnell
Priscilla Young
Jan Zak
Marianne Zinzarella

Chefs and Restaurants:

Fran Babcock, Sarah Kendall House Bed and Breakfast
Richard and Claudette Brodeur, Aaron Smith Farm
Raphael Conte, Bar·Risto
Jaime D'Oliveira, Capital Grille
Gaetano D'Urso, Capriccio Restaurant
1811 House, Manchester, Vermont
Jack and Marcia Felber, Olympia Tea Room
David Gaudet, La France Restaurant
James Griffin and Christine Stamm, Johnson & Wales University
Brant and Eileen Heckert, Pastiche Fine Desserts
Fabrizio Iannucci, Il Piccolo and Pizzico Restaurants
George Karousos, Sea Fare Inn
Leslie Kellogg, Leslie Kellogg Fine Foods
Greg Maser and Michael Bradley, Hospital Trust Bank
Michael Moskwa, Johnson and Wales University
Paul O'Connell, Providence Restaurant, Brookline, Massachusetts
Pauldon's Gourmet Express Catering
Peleg Arnold's Tavern
Walter Potenza, Sunflower Cafe
Rue de l'espoir
Judy Rush, International Gourmet Society
Sconset Cafe, Nantucket, Massachusetts
Sprague Mansion
Louise Wilcox, Citizens Bank

Index of Recipes